Representations of Lethal Gender-Based Violence in Italy Between Journalism and Literature

I0825961

This book discusses femicide in Italy, and the cultural conversations that have resulted from feminist discourse on lethal violence against women entering the mainstream, by analyzing journalistic inquiries and literary works produced after 2012.

In a global and national context where activism's goals are mainly discursive, this study deepens our understanding of the role played by written narratives in the critique of a public interest matter such as gender-based violence. The first part of the book is dedicated to the analysis of three journalistic inquiries published in book format that focus on one or more cases of femicide that happened on the Italian peninsula. The second section draws on the concept of feminist rewriting to propose the analysis of a heterogeneous body of literary texts that explore some of the most controversial and notorious femicide cases covered by previous journalistic, historical, or mythical narratives, before demonstrating the close connection between theoretical and narrative discourse within the analyzed texts.

This is a fascinating case study contributing to global understandings of gender-based violence, which will be important for researchers in gender studies, sociology, and media studies.

Nicoletta Mandolini is FCT researcher at CECS, Universidade do Minho, Portugal. At CECS, she works on the project "Sketch That Story and Make It Popular" using Graphic Narratives in Italian and Lusophone Feminist Activism Against Gender Violence (www.sketchthatstory.com). She was previously FWO postdoctoral researcher at KU Leuven, Belgium, and received her PhD from University College Cork, Ireland. Funded by the Irish Research Council, her doctorate project focused on the representation of gender-based violence and feminicide in contemporary Italian journalistic and literary narratives. She is coeditor of *Rappresentare la violenza di genere. Sguardi femministi tra critica, attivismo e scrittura* (2018), and the author of several articles.

Focus on Global Gender and Sexuality

https://www.routledge.com/Focus-on-Global-Gender-and-Sexuality/book-series/FGGS

Trans Dilemmas
Stephen Kerry

Gender, Sport, and the Role of the Alter Ego in Roller Derby
Colleen E. Arendt

The Poetry of Arab Women from the Pre-Islamic Age to Andalusia
Wessam Elmeligi

Interviews with Mexican Women
We Don't Talk About Feminism Here
Carlos M. Coria-Sanchez

Pornography, Indigeneity, and Neocolonialism
Tim Gregory

Reading Iraqi Women's Novels in English Translation
Iraqi Women's Stories
Ruth Abou Rached

Gender Hierarchy of Masculinity and Femininity during the Chinese Cultural Revolution
Revolutionary Opera Films
Zhuying Li

Representations of Lethal Gender-Based Violence in Italy Between Journalism and Literature
Femminicidio Narratives
Nicoletta Mandolini

Representations of Lethal Gender-Based Violence in Italy Between Journalism and Literature

Femminicidio Narratives

Nicoletta Mandolini

LONDON AND NEW YORK

First published 2022
by Routledge
2 Park Square, Milton Park, Abingdon, Oxon OX14 4RN

and by Routledge
605 Third Avenue, New York, NY 10158

Routledge is an imprint of the Taylor & Francis Group, an informa business

British Library Cataloguing-in-Publication Data
A catalogue record for this book is available from the British Library

Library of Congress Cataloging-in-Publication Data
Names: Mandolini, Nicoletta, author.
Title: Representations of lethal gender-based violence in Italy : between journalism and literature : femminicidio narratives / Nicoletta Mandolini.
Description: Abingdon, Oxon ; New York : Routledge, 2022. | Includes bibliographical references and index. |
Identifiers: LCCN 2021016225 (print) | LCCN 2021016226 (ebook) | ISBN 9780367636975 (hardback) | ISBN 9780367636999 (paperback) | ISBN 9781003120339 (ebook) | ISBN 9781000424898 (adobe pdf) | ISBN 9781000424942 (epub)
Subjects: LCSH: Journalism--Italy--History--21st century. | Crime and the press--Italy--History--21st century. | Murder--Press coverage--Italy. | Women--Crimes against--Italy--Press coverage. | Murder--Italy--Case studies. | Women--Crimes against--Italy--Case studies. | Feminist criminology.
Classification: .LCC PN5244 .M34 2022 (print) | LCC PN5244 (ebook) | DDC 075.09/05--dc23.
LC record available at https://lccn.loc.gov/2021016225.
LC ebook record available at https://lccn.loc.gov/2021016226

ISBN: 978-0-367-63697-5 (hbk)
ISBN: 978-0-367-63699-9 (pbk)
ISBN: 978-1-003-12033-9 (ebk)

DOI: 10.4324/9781003120339

Typeset in Times New Roman
by MPS Limited, Dehradun

To the woman who gave me courage and voice: my mother

Contents

Acknowledgments

This book is the result of a long study that I could conduct with financial ease thanks to the funding allocated by the Irish Research Council (IRC), by the Research Foundation Flanders (FWO), and by the Portuguese Fundação para a Ciência e a Tecnologia (FCT).

I wish to thank many people who supported me and my project, both at an intellectual and emotional level. This book was conceived and researched during the five long years I spent at University College Cork (Ireland), where I had the pleasure to participate in the activities of the research cluster on Violence, Conflict, and Gender, embedded in the Centre for Advanced Studies in Languages and Cultures (CASiLaC). The group granted me vital intellectual exchange and encouragement. Special thanks to Caroline Williamson Sinalo, with whom I co-convened the group and friendly collaborated on numerous projects. Thanks to Nuala Finnegan, Cêire Broderick, Chiara Bonfiglioli, Adelina Syms, Emer Clifford, Vittorio Bufacchi, Alan Gibbs, David Fitzgerald, and Theresa O'Keefe. I am sincerely grateful to the Department of Italian at University College Cork. Many thanks to all the fantastic colleagues at the School of Languages, Literatures, and Cultures.

This writing project benefited enormously from the reading and mentorship of Silvia Ross, Stefania Lucamante, Daragh O'Connell, Marco Amici, Alessia Risi. Thanks to Annette Feeney, who looked after my English while I was busy learning Portuguese. Thanks to Inge Lanslots, Barbara Siller, Alfredo Luzi, Carla Carotenuto, Marina Bettaglio, Martina Piperno, Valeria Venditti, Giovanni Pietro Vitali, Gabriella Caponi, Sara Lis Ventura, Davide Boerio, Antonio Lunardi, Michele Ronchi Stefanati, Mariangela Sanese, Jacopo Turini: they were all precious interlocutors during the many phases of this research.

Thanks to Anna Pramstrahler and the amazing women who allowed me to visit the shelter and feminist association Casa delle donne per non subire violenza in Bologna. Thanks to the activists of the Casa internazionale delle donne, who welcomed me during a research trip in Rome.

Thanks to my beautiful friends: Claudia, Elena, Maria Laura, Valentina, Serena, Marco, Daniele, Peter, Luca, Roberto, Mattia.

Infinite thanks to Valeria, who knows better than me that there's more to sisterhood than a bunch of common chromosomes.

Thanks to the polar star of all my wanderings, my family: my mother Cinzia, my sisters Margherita and Valentina (I would have chosen them anyway, notwithstanding the chromosomes), my niece Clara, my father Maurizio. My beloved grandmother Dea, who passed away in the last days of this writing process.

A special thought for the women who lost their lives in their struggle against patriarchal violence. This book is proof of my commitment to continuing the fight.

Introduction

Femminicidio in Italy and the ethics of its representation

Femicide and its offshoots in the Italian context

Despite being as old as patriarchy (Radford and Russell 1992:25), the phenomenon of femicide was only isolated as a concept with the publication of the volume *Femicide. The Politics of Woman Killing*, edited by Jill Radford and Diana E. H. Russell in 1992. A groundbreaking work in the field of feminist studies against gender-based violence, Radford and Russell's text revived a term already used in the English vocabulary and employed it to identify forms of misogynous abuse that result in a woman's death (Radford 1992:3). The naming operation aimed at introducing a political category that could expand the international criminological spectrum to overcome the universalizing concept that lies behind the term homicide, which obliterates women's particular experience of lethal violence (3). Statistics show that women and girls are generally murdered in contexts and circumstances that differ significantly if compared to killings where the victim is a man. In fact, the majority of women killed worldwide are murdered by intimate (mostly male) partners or family members (UNWomen 2020), which indicates that female victimization is inextricably linked to the highly gendered dynamics that regulate familial and sentimental relationships in our patriarchal societies. The intention to recognize lethal violence against women as a byproduct of sexist oppression guided Radford and Russell's work, as demonstrated by Radford's reference (1992:3) to the "continuum of sexual violence," an idea developed by Liz Kelly (1987) to emphasize the common ground (patriarchal culture) from which different types of abuses suffered by women (e.g. rape, domestic violence, sexual harassment) emerge.

The notion of femicide circulated widely in feminist circles and the term was semantically expanded by scholars and activists such as Nedera Shalhoub-Kevorkian (2003), who labeled as femicide acts that

DOI: 10.4324/9781003120339-101

despite not resulting in death, cause the physical and psychological annihilation of the woman. A further contribution was made by the Mexican anthropologist Marcela Lagarde y de los Ríos, who introduced the Spanish word *feminicidio* to refer to the killings that happened in the northern Mexican region of Chihuahua, where, since 1993, hundreds of women and girls died or disappeared in the area of Ciudad Juárez, a border city located near El Paso, Texas. Lagarde's concept, shaped in the context of political activism against a massive occurrence of sexist violence, retrieves the idea of femicide as non-exclusively lethal violence (2006:66) and functions as a sociological category in which the killing of a woman is not considered a single act but rather a part of a widespread phenomenon that equates to genocide (2010:xiii–xiv). Nowadays, the category of femicide is used worldwide in policies, law, and research to describe the most extreme form of gendered violence against women and girls (e.g. General Assembly 2012a:6; ACUNS 2012, 2014; EIGE 2017; Canadian Femicide Observatory for Justice and Accountability 2018; Shalva et al. 2018).

In 2012, following an invitation from the Italian government, the United Nations special rapporteur on violence against women, Rashida Manjoo, undertook a mission to Italy. The mission, which resulted in a detailed report (General Assembly 2012b), aimed to examine the local situation of gender-related abuse and dedicated a part to the issue of femicide, a crime on the rise in the peninsula at the time. This event testifies to a new interest in the problem of lethal sexist violence, which can be drawn back to the mainstreaming of the feminist discourse on femicide that happened in Italy in 2012.

Feminist discussions on femicide in the Italian peninsula started in 2006, when the association Giuristi Democratici [Democratic Lawyers] published the handbook *Violenza sulle donne: parliamo di femminicidio* [Violence Against Women: Let's Talk about Femicide], which was followed, in 2008, by Barbara Spinelli's book *Femminicidio. Dalla denuncia sociale al riconoscimento giuridico internazionale* [Femicide. From Social Denunciation to International Juridical Recognition]. Giuristi Democratici's and Spinelli's work had the merit to import international theorizations on femicide in the Italian context and, consequently, to introduce the word *femminicidio*,[1] which was subsequently used in a feminist demonstration against gender violence organized in Rome in 2007 (Bandettini 2007) and, just one year after, during a trial in Perugia for the killing of Barbara Cicioni (Spinelli 2008:165). Dictionaries started registering the inclusion of the neologisms *femminicidio* and *femicidio* in the Italian vocabulary between 2007 and 2009 (Paoli 2013). The term left the niche of feminist discourse in 2012, as shown by scholarly works that observed its massive adoption by Italian journalists in the coverage of murder cases with women as victims (Bandelli and Porcelli 2016:13–14), as well as its introduction in the area of political debates (Laviosa 2015:6), in the blogosphere (Mandolini 2017:361), and in literature (Mandolini 2019:172). The process of mainstreaming the feminist concept of *femminicidio* resulted in an intensive and extensive presence of the neologism in the Italian communicative sphere, which permits the Italian discussion on femicide to be labeled as a "discursive event" (Jäger and Maier 2009:48–49). As such, the debate had the capacity to impact more general discursive practices, as well as to act on the subversion of societal power relationships. This is confirmed by the concomitant presence of crucial political events such as the ratification in September 2012 of the Council of Europe's Istanbul Convention on preventing and combating violence against women, followed by the decision to promulgate a national law on femicide in October 2013.[2]

The relevance that the topic of lethal gender violence[3] reached in the Italian context is not common and it can only be compared to the popularity that the concept of *feminicidio* attained in the Spanish-speaking world in the wake of the previously mentioned killings of Ciudad Juárez (Mandolini 2017:360). The interest in the issue is not the result of a particularly high rate of femicides afflicting the country, on the contrary, it is the outcome of the arduous effort undertaken by feminist activists who succeeded in assigning public importance to a vicious phenomenon that was previously ignored by national discourse. Available data show that femicide in Italy is an alarming fact whose persistence illustrates the situation of gender inequality that characterizes Italian society. However, numbers are not high, if compared to those of other countries. According to a study carried out by the Bolognese women's shelter Casa delle donne per non subire violenza, 1,428 women were killed for gender-related reasons from 2008 to 2019 (Femicidio 2020). Another study undertaken by ISTAT, the Italian institute for statistical research, shows a significant general decrease in the number of homicides with male victims and a worrying consistency in the number of killings of women, which testifies to institutional and societal failure to tackle gender-related crimes (ISTAT 2020). Notwithstanding this, in 2018, the rate of murders with women as victims in Italy (0.43 per 100,000 women) was lower than the European Union average (0.70 per 100,000 women) (ISTAT 2020), while in 2006 Italy had a percentage of 5.64 femicides per million, which was lower than that of countries such as Germany (9.20), Norway (8.25), England and Wales (7.73) (Sanmartin Espulgues et al. 2010:67–68).

The discursive prominence of femicide in Italy can be associated with the emergence of a new wave of feminist movements in the years that coincide with the last phase of the Berlusconi era (1994–2011), when women started to denounce the systematic process of objectification to which feminine bodies were subjected in national television and political discourse. This phase, which ended with the infamous scandal of the *Bunga Bunga* – an expression used to label the sex parties organized by the prime minister Silvio Berlusconi in 2010 – resulted in the formation of feminist associations and networks that contributed to reinvigorate the national discussion on gender-related issues and shed light on the mechanisms of discrimination that affected Italian women.[4] This brought the circulation of criticisms on issues that dominated – and still dominate – Italian society, such as the hypersexualization of women, the chronic underrepresentation of women in employment and in politics, the widespread practice of abusing feminine subjects in the streets and in the home, as well as the persistence of rigid gender roles in the household and in the workplace (General Assembly 2012b:6).

The temporal concurrence with the 2012 mainstreaming of the discourse on femicide demonstrates the ability of Italian feminist groups to undertake an effective holistic reflection that has examined the spheres of public and private life where symbolic and direct violence interconnect. In light of this, the effort to bring to the fore a discussion on intimate partner killings (the most common form of femicide in Italy) can be interpreted as a fortunate attempt to project a phenomenon that was previously underdiscussed and not addressed at a political level into the realm of a public discourse that was demonstrating an increasing interest in gender issues. This was the first time that Italian feminist movements succeeded in attributing major media resonance to the extreme consequences of the most private of gender-based violence typologies: domestic violence and abuse between intimate partners. Previous achievements in raising public awareness on the issue of sexist abuse were mainly connected to the politicization of rapes and murders committed by strangers (Pitch 2008:7). This is the case of the Circeo massacre, which consisted in the kidnapping, vexation, and repeated rape of Rosaria Lopez (who was also killed) and Donatella Colasanti (who survived) by Angelo Izzo, Gianni Guido, and Andrea Ghira. The Circeo massacre happened in September 1975 in the outskirts of Rome and caused a wave of political discussions on sexual violence. The violation and killing of Giovanna Reggiani at the hands of Naicolae Mailat, which happened in a Roma camp in 2007, is another case that reverberated widely in Italian media and political discourse.[5]

Italian feminist movements' current capacity to consider the denunciation of femicide crucial to the recognition of the private sphere as a privileged site for the maintenance of gender abuses is furtherly confirmed by the creation, in 2016, of the feminist network Non una di meno, which borrowed its name from the Argentinian anti femicide group Ni una menos [No one left]. Starting with the condemnation of lethal gender violence, it launched a series of campaigns aimed at confronting more general types of gender discrimination.[6] Possibly the most influential social movement in contemporary Italy, Non una di meno is the emblem of a country that is finally compelling its public opinion to face the deadly consequences of everyday patriarchal injustices.

Femminicidio narratives

The political and theoretical debate on femicide was complemented by the production of journalistic and literary narratives that helped in the process of popularization of feminist theories and contributed to the improvement of the public's level of awareness of the phenomenon. The daily press, for example, has frequently reported on cases of lethal gender violence that, before 2012, journalists did not even recognize as specific (Giomi 2015:569–570). Concurrently, investigative journalism provided Italian readers with in-depth inquiries on the general phenomenon or on particular cases of femicide. These productions, which are mostly characterized by the presence of a subjective and explicitly positioned narrative voice, constitute the necessary link between the apparent objectivity of daily journalistic narratives and a tendency in literary texts toward a narration of the non-documentable. On the literary front, Italian authors have published, since 2012, numerous works that directly or indirectly denounce the issue of femicide.

The narration of femicide is a necessary act whose potential lies in supporting the circulation of feminist insights on sexist violence. However, the representation of lethal gender violence is a risky practice because its implementation is filled with ethical challenges, and its objective needs to be twofold. On the one hand, it should contribute to overcoming the "violence of rhetoric" that for centuries obliterated women's experiences of victimization (de Lauretis 1987:34). On the other, representations of gender abuse should reduce the risks associated with the process that Teresa de Lauretis labeled "rhetoric of violence," (1987:34) which is the inevitable manipulation implied in the practice of adapting a complex and polymorphous reality to the authorial subject's expressive limitations. A failure to do so would contribute to discursive processes of exclusion and normalization, as well as to the reproduction of the symbolic dynamics of oppression that legitimize patriarchal hierarchies.

Feminist representations of femicide are almost invariably characterized by the common intention to give voice or narrative space to those who no longer have a voice: women silenced by patriarchal abuse. However, the laudable intention to reassign protagonism to subjects who have been violently deprived of their personhood (Adamo and Bertoni 2003:8) might result in problematic narrative acts. In this regard, the most critical aspect is the danger of appropriating the victim's testimonial need. Considering that authors who decide to narrate femicide cannot coincide with the represented victimized subject, their narrative practice runs the risk of being interpreted as a further violence toward the murdered woman who ends up becoming the object of someone else's rhetorical operation. As a result, feminist narratives on lethal gender violence are tied to specific ethical limitations concerning the author's positioning and – in case of works based on true events – the tale's adherence to facts.

On these topics, feminist scholars have emphasized the need to question the radical epistemological approach proposed by poststructuralist philosophy, which considers social reality an exclusively discursive entity. In particular, de Lauretis alerted to uncritical feminist uses of Foucauldian theories and contended that, despite the crucial role that these insights have had in the process of denouncing the connection between discourse and domination, they do not take into account the fundamental role played by embodied experience in the social construction of gender hierarchies (1987:38). With the aim of reassigning a concrete dimension to women's experience of discrimination and violence, de Lauretis proposed to integrate Foucauldian reflections on discourse with those elaborated by the semiotician Charles Sanders Peirce, who considered the physical world and empirical reality relevant to the process of representation (38–42). In light of this, a reference to the theories proposed by Kory Spencer Sorrell, a feminist and Peircian philosopher whose work aims at overcoming the limitations of poststructuralist thought, is useful to understand the risks connected to the representation of femicide in the Italian context and beyond.

Sorrell argues that no representative act is able to integrally reproduce the composite and dynamic stratifications of reality; therefore, representation cannot be but a process of approximation (2004:156), and no narrative can be entirely objective or truthful. However, representations on a socially relevant topic such as gender violence cannot evade a dialog with the reality of the female experience of victimization. For this reason, authors should respond to a double commitment: to declare the inevitable partiality of their operation (their positioning), and to adopt an inclusive gaze aimed at minimizing the risks connected to their epistemological prejudice by means of a steady confrontation with the complexities of reality (Sorrell 2004:148–149).

If feminist narratives on femicide have the objective of reaffirming the relevance of women's struggle against violence, a positioning that coincides with the female gender would be desirable given its potential ability to challenge traditional patriarchal authori(ali)ty (Sniader Lanser 1992:6). On the contrary, a male gender positioning would be inevitably problematic because of its implicit association with the historically documented tendency of male voices to assimilate, and consequently obliterate, women's (hi)story of abuse. Notwithstanding this, situated narratives whose authors identify with the male gender could offer a feminist representation of femicide if they provide the reader with a critical reflection on the issue of toxic masculinity, thus questioning the teller's gender privilege.

The author's positioning is made possible by the employment of an explicitly subjective narrative. Subjective narrative styles are traditionally linked to literary writing, but they are generally considered inappropriate or eccentric if used in journalistic accounts. According to the antinomy that regulates the canonical distinction between the two writing typologies, journalism tends to impersonality and objectivity; literature, on the contrary, reshapes reality on the basis of the creative operation carried out by the writer (Bertoni 2009:6). In Italy, this distinction has weakened since the 1990s, when journalists have started to adopt subjective rhetorical strategies borrowed from literature (Buonanno 1999). However, in the case of many journalistic accounts, subjective narration is not presented as such and is made invisible by the absence of clear statements on the author's positioning, which contributes to the misleading reception of the narrative as objective. This lack of opaqueness is problematic when it comes to representations of true stories of femicide (nonfictional portrayals) as it conceals the inevitable process of the appropriation of the victim's violent experience.

This is not the case with fictional literary narratives, where the lack of a direct relationship with real events allows the author more freedom. Moreover, authorial positioning is implicit to the process of fictional composition, given the reader's automatic recognition of the writer's creativity as a constitutive dimension in literary practice. For this same reason, the author's gender is not a strictly limiting element in fictions on femicide. As Rita Felski pointed out, essentialist statements on the masculine or feminine dimension of literary writings should be avoided, as "the political value of literary texts from the standpoint of feminism can be determined only by an investigation of their social functions and effects in relation to the interests of women in a particular historical context." (1989:2) What counts, in the case of literary narratives that are not based on true events, is their narratological positioning, which, traditionally, does not coincide with that of the author of fiction. In this sense, preferable texts are centered on a female perspective. Alternatively, they adopt a male narratological point of view that critically reflects on gender privilege.

Both in the case of fictional and non-fiction works, a multidimensional and non-stereotypical representation of the victim is a necessary requirement for feminist narratives on femicide. The practice of providing a stratified portrayal of the victim complies with a feminist ethics of representation that refuses the reduction of femininity to the rigid categorizations offered by patriarchal discourse, such as the infamous dichotomies that divide women between virgins and whores (Benedict 1992; Millett 1969:190–194) or between passive/fragile individuals and subjects to blame. More importantly, simplified depictions of the victim offered in the context of non-fictional narratives reduce the woman's personhood to generalizations that the author might use to compensate the lack of direct experience determined by her/his external positioning. This practice is inherently linked to the process of narrating someone else's story, thus being inevitable to some degree. However, it should be limited at the least and balanced by the authors' effort to conduct research that prevents them from being detrimental to the image of the victim's subjectivity.

The traps of gender dichotomization

As already mentioned, the adoption of the concept of femicide needs to be referred to a feminist operation that considers women's victimization one of the consequences of a patriarchal social and symbolic order. Which is to say that femicide highlights the difference that separates men's and women's experiences of lethal abuse. This difference, which is inextricably linked to the existence of gender-based relationships of domination (Kelly 1987; Goldner et al. 1990), is the real and statistically confirmed phenomenon from which all feminist narratives on femicide start. In other words, representations of violence against women cannot abstain from describing the system of gender oppositions that has historically determined women's discrimination and coercion (de Lauretis 1987:37–38).

Yet portrayals of phenomena like femicide should not rely on an exclusively descriptive approach if they want to contribute to the modification of the patriarchal discursive structure that guarantees the continuation of the social practice of gender violence. According to the sociologist Pierre Bourdieu, gender inequalities are sustained through the reproduction of a dichotomous system of thought that constructs masculinity and femininity and establishes a hierarchy between the two by assigning to each category specific characteristics. For example, masculinity is associated with domination and strength, while femininity is linked to ideas of subjugation and weakness. Patriarchal discourse naturalizes this hierarchy, thus perpetuating that symbolic violence that legitimizes concrete gender abuse (Bourdieu 2002:7–11). This symbolic order can be overturned only by means of a discursive turmoil "aimed at imposing new categories of perception and appreciation, so as to [...] destroy the very principle of division through which the stigmatizing group and the stigmatized group are produced." (123)

Similarly, the feminist psychoanalyst Jessica Benjamin argued that sexist domination of a gender over the other stems from the crystallization of the cultural opposition between masculinity and femininity, which reproduces the dichotomy subject vs object and results in the impossibility of mutual recognition and equality (1990:220). An intersubjective space where the two parts (masculinity and femininity, subject and object) ideally meet, see each other as interdependent entities, and abandon the hierarchical polarization is, for Benjamin, the only dimension in which the relationship of domination can be sabotaged (1990:220).

Bourdieu's and Benjamin's theories confirm that patriarchal domination, from which the phenomenon of femicide originates, is strictly linked to the conservation of psychosocial and symbolic dynamics that insist on gender binarisms. Therefore, the attempt to overcome on a discursive level the dichotomization between masculinity and femininity, together with the effort to unveil the cultural dimension of the opposition between man-perpetrator and woman-victim, should supplement the denunciation of existing gender hierarchies. In other words, feminist narratives on lethal gender violence have the twofold responsibility of describing and at the same time rhetorically contesting the dichotomous symbolic system that supports gender abuse.

Overcoming spectacularization, promoting identification

In *Regarding the Pain of the Others* (2003), Susan Sontag provides her readers with an illuminating analysis of the risks connected to the use of photographic images that reproduce scenes of brutalities or death. Notwithstanding the different object of analysis (war violence) and the different medium analyzed (photography), Sontag's reflections can be borrowed to discuss the issue of the narrative exposition of the femicide event and its ethical controversies. According to the philosopher, the process of reproducing images of lethal violence could result in the spectacularization of suffering, whose negative moral consequences could exceed the positive repercussions of denouncing atrocities (Sontag 2003:63–70). This possibility is particularly relevant in the case of portrayals of gender abuse if we take into account the historically subaltern role of female subjects in the area of mass media representation, where feminine bodies are often reified or eroticized (Gallagher 1981:38–39) and where even their victimization is an object of glamourization (Stankiewicz and Rosselli 2008; Foltyn 2011).

In light of these considerations, spectacularization of violence (which is to say, a representation that attracts or entertains the viewer/reader by means of the exhibition of scenes of brutality) is a detrimental practice that contributes to the visual/narrative exploitation of the sufferer and to the reproduction of gender stereotypes. Moreover, spectacularizing portrayals indirectly encourage receivers to occupy the detached position of the spectator (Sontag 2003:85–86), which, as Guy Debord pointed out in his famous theorizations on the spectacle, perceives herself/himself as separated from the represented object or phenomenon (2014:2–11). This inhibits the receivers' capacity of identification with the narrative, thus invalidating the whole representative process that, in the case of portrayals of femicide, should lead to the stimulation of the reader's comprehension of patriarchal abuse's pervasive and familiar nature.

Identification is, in fact, quite the opposite of spectacularization. If spectacular representations are based on the detailed depiction of violent scenes that trigger the receivers' superficial reaction but do not leave space for their actual participation in the creation of meaning, identification, according to the German scholar Wolfgang Iser, is determined by the presence, in the text, of unresolved details or fruitful omissions. These gaps guarantee the constant interaction between the work and the receivers, who are implicitly asked to fill the breaches by means of an imaginary effort that results in deep engagement (Iser 1972:280–281). It is precisely by virtue of their active role that readers connect with the narrated events even when these are not directly related to their previous life experiences (283).

But, for Iser, identification is just a means through which the text acts on the readers' imagined life experiences and influences their imaginary. Identification, in other words, is not enough. In order to modify the receivers' imaginary, identification needs to be coupled with another process associated to the act of reading: the betrayal of the horizon of expectations. First used in literary studies by Iser's colleague Hans Robert Jauss, the expression horizon of expectations describes the anticipations that readers inevitably produce before approaching or while reading a text. These anticipations can be related to the style of the text or to its contribution to a specific cultural or political cause (Jauss 1982:23), but they can also result from the aforementioned textual omissions or from the presence of simple textual pauses (Iser 1972:283). When readers are forced to interrupt their flow of reading, they have no choice but to creatively overcome the gap with anticipations that might be subsequently betrayed by the text itself, which demands readers to renegotiate their assumptions and perspectives (282–284). This constant dialog between the reader and the literary work consists in the reorientation from the familiar toward the non-familiar or in other words, in the systematic dismantlement of prejudices that allows the reading subject to open herself/himself to new experiences and imaginaries (295).

Iserian theories on identification were confirmed by Umberto Eco, who suggested that authors always compose narrative texts having a model reader in mind, who is ideally able to fill the blank spaces by making reference to her/his encyclopedic knowledge, as well as to her/his ability of making inferences (1979:51–55). According to the Italian semiologist, narratives are crowded with elements that stimulate the receivers to produce a probability disjunction (113), which is the process of making conjectures based on common sense and typical situations (117–119). If consolatory narratives confirm the readers' inferences, witty texts disregard them and leave the plot partially unresolved. The latter textual typology, which is labeled by Eco as open work, supports multiple interpretations and is characterized by an eminently entropic ethics that stimulates the participation of those who read by forcing them into an act of creative and unsettling reflection (1987:41–43).

Iser and Eco's intuitions on the interdependence of identification and innovation are crucial to the analysis of representations of femicide. On the one hand, identification guarantees the assimilation of the perturbing experience of violence and gender-based conflict in the realm of the receiver's imaginary, thus contributing to the development of a deep and intimate awareness on the phenomenon. On the other, textual openness and the productive practice of betraying the reader's horizon of expectation support the process of overcoming the stereotypical and dichotomous thinking on which patriarchal discourse is based.

This book

The book investigates the impact of mainstreaming feminist discourse on written narratives of femicide produced in Italy since 2012. Considering banalization as one of the risks linked to the widespread dissemination of feminist insights on gender-based violence (Boyle 2005:84–92), the main objective of the volume is to analyze the texts' ability to popularize theories on femicide through the use of narrative techniques that appeal a general audience without diminishing the complexity of the feminist message. The presence in the text of a clear authorial positioning, the capacity of the work to describe and at the same time overcome gender hierarchies, and the author's effort to avoid spectacularization and promote identification are the criteria according to which the narratives will be read and evaluated.

Representations of Lethal Gender-Based Violence in Italy Between Journalism and Literature: Femminicidio *Narratives* consists of two parts dedicated to the analysis of journalistic inquiries and literary works. Part 1, "Journalistic Inquiries on *Femminicidio*," begins with chapter 1, "Beyond the Principle of Objective Narrative," which presents the themes that have dominated the Italian discussions on the media portrayal of lethal gender violence (alternatively labeled as metadiscourse on femicide) and connects them to the production of journalistic narratives that focus on one or more cases of femicide that occurred on the Italian peninsula. This chapter also introduces the reader to the growing tendency of journalistic works to include fictional and emotional modes and registers (Buonanno 1999:58–62) with the aim of identifying the influence that this propensity has had on the portrayal of an ethically delicate phenomenon such as femicide. Chapter 2, "*Il sangue delle donne* (2014) by Alvaro Fiorucci," analyzes a journalistic inquiry that includes 64 accounts of murder cases where the victims of violence were women or girls. The study of Fiorucci's work provides readers with the example of a text that makes implicit references to feminist discourse on femicide but relies on a supposedly objective and highly stereotypical narrative style that often revictimizes the killed women, thus ultimately failing to align with the feminist representative ethos. Chapter 3, "*Se questi sono gli uomini* (2012) by Riccardo Iacona," reads a reportage written by a famous television journalist and presenter on femicides that took place in Italy in 2012. The analysis, which insists on the explicitly male narratological position proposed by Iacona, identifies in the intersubjective dimension of the text its ability to establish an emotional bond with the receivers and to raise awareness on the specific issue of toxic masculinity. However, it also highlights the heteronormative dimension of the narration. Chapter 4, "*Quello che resta* (2013) by Serena Maiorana" focuses on a hybrid journalistic inquiry conducted on the femicide case of Stefania Noce, which happened in Sicily in December 2011. The explicitly victim-centered perspective adopted by the woman journalist to narrate the intimate partner killing and reassign dignity to the figure of Noce successfully avoids stereotypical and idealizing portrayals but offers a problematic unidimensional representation of the perpetrator.

Part 2, "Literary Re-Writings of *Femminicidio* Narratives," analyzes a heterogeneous body of literary texts that explore some of the most controversial and notorious femicide stories covered by previous journalistic, historical, or mythical narratives with the aim of discussing the discrepancy between accounts of femicide based on true events and creative narratives on the topic. Chapter 5, "Between Fiction and Non-Fiction. Femicide in Italian Literature," identifies the main features that characterize literary narratives on lethal gender violence in the Italian context. By making reference to the key concept of feminist rewriting (Plate 2011) this chapter also introduces the corpus of works selected for the study and offers a brief reading of non-fictional and fictional representations of sexist abuse published on the peninsula before 2012. Chapter 6, "Rewriting Journalistic Narratives. *Fiore…come me* (2013) by Giuliana Covella and *Nessuna più* (2013), edited by Marilù Oliva," compares two short-story collections based on journalistic accounts of recently committed femicides. The presence of significant differences both in the curatorial choices that concern the authorial positioning and in the thematic representations of victims and perpetrators demonstrates the possibility of two different and, to some extent, opposed ways of recuperating true stories of femicide from newspaper reports. Chapter 7, "Rewriting History. *La scuola cattolica* (2016) by Edoardo Albinati," analyzes the critically acclaimed autofictional retelling of the Circeo massacre with the aim of examining the ethical issues that arise from the representation, with specific reference to the puzzling relationship that the perpetrator-centered text and the ambiguous truthfulness of the male-based authorial voice establish with the reality of women's victimization. It identifies in Albinati's novel a reluctance to give voice to the victims while at the same time recognizing a tendency to tone down the male voice and, with it, the whole gender dichotomy from which gender violence stems. Chapter 8, "Rewriting the Myth. *Padreterno* (2015) by Caterina Serra," reads an entirely fictional narrative that uses the classical myth of Aristaeus as intertext to create a story of gender lethal violence and redemption. By making reference to Jessica Benjamin's theorizations on the idea of thirdness (2018:24), this chapter identifies in the utopic realm of literature the space where the possibility of overcoming gender polarizations materializes.

Despite resulting from the necessary exclusion of other narrative productions on the topic, the selection of works analyzed in this volume is a representative sample that includes texts written both by male and female authors, texts that adopt different narratological perspectives (that of the victim, that of the perpetrator, that of bystanders or external characters), texts that received disparate critical responses and attracted distinct typologies of readers. For this reason, it offers the opportunity to shed a light on the discursive dynamics that in Italy regulate the production of journalistic inquiries and literary works on femicide, as well as on their relationship with the popularization of feminist discourse. Far from being a mere scholarly exercise, this research operation is a necessary step in the process of acquiring knowledge on how gender violence is represented and consequently perceived in Italy and beyond. To adapt Sorche Gunne and Zoe Brigley Thompson's statement on rape and its portrayals (2010:3) to the area of lethal gender violence, now that we have learned to talk about femicide, we need to understand how we do that. Only then we can produce further change.

Notes

1 In Italian, *femminicidio* is a neologism derived from the Spanish term *feminicidio*, which was introduced by Marcela Lagarde to adapt the Anglophone word femicide to the Mexican context, where lethal violence against women have had the characteristics of a genocide. Spinelli preferred to use *femminicidio* over the term *femicidio* (a direct calque from Radford and Russell's concept) because of the broader meaning and higher level of inclusiveness that the Spanish term conveys.

2 The law – Legge 15 ottobre 2013 n. 119 – was not well received by Italian feminists, who criticized its predominantly repressive outlook, the lack of funding it allocates for gender violence prevention, and rhetorical choices such as the employment of the expression "weak subjects" in relation to the victims (Spinelli 2013; Occhiogrosso 2014; Virgilio 2014; Donadi 2015). Notwithstanding these criticisms, the promulgation of the law is testimony to the impact that the discourse on femicide has had in the political sphere.

3 Karen Boyle pointed out that the expressions "gender violence" and "violence against women" cannot be treated as equivalents. "Gender violence" emphasizes the motivations that lead to the violent act and includes abuses carried out against male subjects who do not conform to the model offered by hegemonic masculinity, as well as abuses with transgender and non-binary victims. "Violence against women," on the other hand, highlights the victim's gender or sex and is used to label forms of violence toward female subjects that are not necessarily ascribable to the influence of patriarchal culture (Boyle 2019).

In other words, "violence against women" conceals the gender dimension, while "gender violence" does not describe the social hierarchy according to which men are commonly abusers of women victims. Coherently with the centrality that this volume assigns to the gender cultural dimension of femicide, I decided to give preference to the expression "lethal gender violence"/ "lethal gender-based violence" over "lethal violence against women."

4 The event that symbolizes this new awakening is a demonstration organized by the group Se non ora quando [If not now when?] and held in Rome in February 2011. On that occasion, thousands of women occupied the streets of the Italian capital to protest against the spectacularization of femininity promoted by the national government and media.

5 Both these cases can be labeled as femicides if we consider that lethal gender violence does not necessarily imply the presence of an existing relationship between victim and perpetrator. However, they were not recognized as such by the Italian media and they lacked that dimension of intimacy or domesticity that only with discussions on femicide post-2012 publicly emerged as a crucial component in the phenomenon of patriarchal abuse.

6 On this, see https://nonunadimeno.wordpress.com/.

Works cited

ACUNS (2012) *Femicide. A Global Issue that Demands Action. Vol. 1*. Vienna: ACUNS.

ACUNS (2014) *Femicide. A Global Issue that Demands Action. Vol. 2*. Vienna: ACUNS.

Adamo, S. and Bertoni, C. (2003) "On Voice and Voicelessness between Literature and Law," in Adamo, S. and Bertoni C. (eds.), *Compar(a)ison*. New York: Peter Lang, pp. 5–10.

Albinati, E. (2016) *La scuola cattolica*. Milan: Rizzoli.

Bandelli, D. and Porcelli, G. (2016) "Femicide in Italy. 'Femminicidio,' Moral Panic and Progressivist Discourse," *Sociologica* 2: https://www.rivisteweb.it/doi/10.2383/85284. Accessed 4 January 2021.

Bandettini, A. (2007) Violenza sulle donne. La strage delle innocenti. *La Repubblica*. November 21: https://www.repubblica.it/2007/11/sezioni/cronaca/violenza-donne/violenza-donne/violenza-donne.html. Accessed 4 January 2021.

Benedict, H. (1992) *Virgin or Vamp. How the Press Covers Sex Crimes*. Cambridge, Massachusetts and London: Harvard University Press.

Benjamin, J. (1990) *The Bonds of Love. Psychoanalysis, Feminism, and the Problem of Domination*. London: Virago.

Benjamin, J. (2018) *Beyond Doer and Done To. Recognition Theory, Intersubjectivity, and the Third*. London and New York: Routledge.

Bertoni, C. (2009) *Letteratura e giornalismo*. Rome: Carocci.

Bourdieu, P. (2002) [1998] *Masculine Domination*. Transl. R. Nice. Bloomington: Stanford University Press.

Boyle, K. (2005) *Media and Violence*. Thousand Oaks: Sage.

Boyle, K. (2019) "What's in a Name? Theorizing the Inter-relationships of Gender and Violence," *Feminist Theory* 20(1):19–36.

Buonanno, M. (1999) *Faction. Soggetti mobili e generi ibridi nel giornalismo italiano degli anni novanta*. Naples: Liguori.

Canadian Femicide Observatory for Justice and Accountability. (2018) *#CallItFemicide. Understanding Gender-Related Killings of Women and Girls in Canada 2018*: https://femicideincanada.ca/callitfemicide.pdf. Accessed 28 January 2021.

Covella, G. (2013) *Fiore… come me. Storie di dieci vite spezzate*. Naples: Spazio Creativo.

Debord, G. (2014) [1967] *The Society of the Spectacle*. Transl. K. Knabb. Berkeley: Bureau of Public Secrets.

de Lauretis, T. (1987) *Technologies of Gender. Essays on Theory, Film, and Fiction*. Bloomington and Indianapolis: Indiana University Press.

Donadi, P. (2015) "I crimini contro le donne e la legge sul femminicidio," *Sociologia del diritto* 1:103–119.

Eco, U. (1979) *Lector in fabula. La cooperazione interpretativa nei testi narrativi*. Milan: Bompiani.

Eco, U. (1987) [1962] *The Open Work*. Transl. A. Cancogni. Cambridge, Massachusetts: Harvard University Press.

EIGE. (2017) *Terminology and Indicators for Data Collection: Rape, Femicide and Intimate Partner Violence*. Vilnius: European Institute for Gender Equality.

Felski, R. (1989) *Beyond Feminist Aesthetics. Feminist Literature and Social Change*. London: Hutchinson Radius.

Femicidio. (2020) I femicidi in Italia: i dati della stampa relative al 2019. *Femicidiocasadonne*. October 19: https://femicidiocasadonne.files.wordpress.com/2020/10/poster-femminicidio-jpg-2019-2.jpg. Accessed 4 January 2021.

Fiorucci, A. (2014) *Il sangue delle donne*. Perugia: Morlacchi.

Foltyn, J. L. (2011) "Corpse Chic: Dead Models and Living Corpses in Fashion Photography," in de Witt-Paul, A. and Crouch, M. (eds.), *Fashion Forward*. Freeland: Inter-Disciplinary Press, pp. 379–391.

Gallagher, M. (1981) *Unequal Opportunities. The Case of Women and the Media*. Paris: Unesco.

General Assembly. (2012a) Report of the Special Rapporteur on Violence Against Women, Its Causes and Consequences, Rashida Manjoo. *Ohchr*. May 23: https://www.ohchr.org/Documents/Issues/Women/A.HRC.20.16_En.pdf. Accessed 3 January 2021.

General Assembly. (2012b) Report of the Special Rapporteur on Violence Against Women, Its Causes and Consequences, Rashida Manjoo. Mission to Italy. *Ohchr*. June 15: https://www.ohchr.org/Documents/HRBodies/HRCouncil/RegularSession/Session20/A-HRC-20-16-Add2_en.pdf. Accessed 3 January 2021.

Giomi, E. (2015) "Tag femminicidio. La violenza letale contro le donne nella stampa italiana," *Problemi dell'informazione* 50(3):549–574.

Giuristi Democratici. (2006) Violenza sulle donne: parliamo di femminicidio. *Giuristidemocratici*. October 5: https://www.staticfiles.it/clients/ggdd/filereposit/posts/2006/10/20061005165857/documents/20061005165857.pdf. Accessed 3 January 2021.

Goldner, V., Penn, P. S. and Walker, M. E. G. (1990) "Violence and Love. Gender Paradoxes in Volatile Attachments," *Family Process* 29:343–364.

Gunne, S. and Brigely Thompson, Z. (2010) "Feminism without Borders: The Potentials and Pitfalls of Retheorizing Rape," in Gunne, S. and Brigley Thompson, Z. (eds.), *Literature and Rape Narratives: Violence and Violation*. New York: Routledge, pp. 1–22.

Iacona, R. (2012) *Il sangue delle donne*. Milan: Chiarelettere.

Iser, W. (1972) "The Reading Process: A Phenomenological Approach," *New Literary History* 3(2):279–299.

ISTAT. (2020) Omicidi di donne. *ISTAT*: https://www.istat.it/it/violenza-sulle-donne/il-fenomeno/omicidi-di-donne. Accessed 4 January 2021.

Jauss, H. R. (1982) [1970] *Toward an Aesthetic of Reception*. Transl. T. Bahti. Minneapolis: University of Minnesota Press.

Jäger, S. and Maier, F. (2009) "Theoretical and Methodological Aspects of Foucauldian Critical Discourse Analysis," in Wodak, R. and Meyer, M. (eds.), *Methods of Critical Discourse Analysis*. Thousand Oaks: Sage, pp. 34–61.

Kelly, L. (1987) "The Continuum of Sexual Violence," in Hanmer J. and Maynard, M. (eds.), *Women, Violence and Social Control*. London: Palgrave, pp. 46–60.

Lagarde y de los Ríos, M. (2006) "Intodución," in Congreso de la Unión, *La violencia feminicida en 10 entidades de la República Mexicana*. Mexico City: Congreso de la Unión, pp. 65–72.

Lagarde y de los Ríos, M. (2010) "Preface: Feminist Keys for Understanding Feminicide: Theoretical, Political, and Legal Construction," in Fragoso, R. L. and Bejarano, C. (eds.), *Terrorizing Women: Feminicide in the Amércas*. Durham and London: Duke University Press, pp. xi–xxv.

Laviosa, F. (2015) "Killing in the Name of Love. Violence Against Women in Italy," *JOMEC Journal* 8: https://jomec.cardiffuniversitypress.org/articles/abstract/10.18573/j.2015.10033/ Accessed 03 January 2021.

Maiorana, S. (2013) *Quello che resta: storia di Stefania Noce, il femminicidio e i diritti delle donne nell'Italia di oggi*. Villaggio Maori Edizioni: Valverde.

Millett, K. (1969) *Sexual Politics*. Urbana and Chicago: University of Illinois Press.

Mandolini, N. (2017) "Politicize and Popularize: The Theoretical Discourse on Femicide in Italian Feminist Blogs," *Journal of Italian Cinema and Media Studies* 5(3):357–373.

Mandolini, N. (2019) "Rivisitare la pratica del 'partire da sé': autofiction al maschile e femminicidio ne *La scuola cattolica* di Edoardo Albinati," *Romance Studies* 37(3–4):171–187.

Occhiogrosso, F. (2014) "La legge sul femminicidio: un'occasione mancata," *Minorigiustizia* 1:148–152.

Oliva, M. (ed.) (2013) *Nessuna più. Quaranta scrittori contro il femminicidio*. Rome: Elliot.

Paoli, M. (2013) Femminicidio: I perché di una parola. *Accademia della Crusca.* May 28: https://accademiadellacrusca.it/it/consulenza/femminicidio-i-perche-di-una-parola/803. Accessed 4 January 2021.

Pitch, T. (2008) "Qualche riflessione sulla violenza maschile contro le donne," *Studi sulla questione criminale* 3(2):7–13.

Plate, L. (2011) *Transforming Memories in Women's Contemporary Rewriting.* New York: Palgrave.

Radford, J. and Russell, D. E. H. (eds.) (1992) *Femicide. The Politics of Woman Killing.* New York: Twayne Publishers.

Radford, J. (1992) "Introduction," in Radford, J. and Russell, D. E. H. (eds.), *Femicide. The Politics of Woman Killing.* New York: Twayne Publishers, pp. 3–12.

Sanmartin Espulgues, J., Iborra Marmolejo, I., García Estevez, Y. and Martínez Sánchez, P. (2010) *3rd International Report. Partner Violence against Women: Statistics and Legislation.* Valencia: Valencian International University.

Serra, C. (2015) *Padreterno.* Turin: Einaudi.

Shalva, W., Corradi, C. and Naudi, M. (2018) *Femicide Across Europe: Theory, Research and Prevention.* Bristol: Policy Press.

Shalhoub-Kevorkian, N. (2003) "Reexamining Femicide: Breaking the Silence and Crossing 'Scientific' Borders," *Signs* 28(2):581–608.

Sniader Lanser, S. (1992) *Fictions of Authority. Women Writers and Narrative Voice.* Ithaca and London: Cornell University Press.

Sontag, S. (2003) *Regarding the Pain of the Others.* London: Picador.

Sorrell, K. S. (2004) *Representative Practices: Pierce, Pragmatism and Feminist Epistemology.* New York: Fordham University Press.

Spinelli, B. (2008) *Femminicidio. Dalla denuncia sociale al riconoscimento giuridico internazionale.* Milan: Franco Angeli.

Spinelli, B. (2013) "Femminicidio e riforme legislative," *Questione giudiziaria* 12:50–61.

Stankiewicz, J. and Rosselli, F. (2008) "Women as Sex Objects and Victims in Print Advertisements," *Sex Roles* 58(7-8):579–589.

UNWomen. (2020) "Facts and Figures: Ending Violence Against Women," *UNWomen.* November 2020: https://www.unwomen.org/en/what-we-do/ending-violence-against-women/facts-and-figures. Accessed 2 January 2021.

Virgilio, M. (2014) "La legge sul femminicidio," *M@gm@* 12.1: http://www.analisiqualitativa.com/magma/1201/articolo_08.htm. Accessed 4 January 2021.

Part I

Journalistic inquiries on *Femminicidio*

1 Beyond the principle of objective narrative

The metadiscourse on the representation of *Femminicidio* in the media

Following the relocation of Italian discussions on femicide from the small niche of feminist discourse to the mainstream media sphere in 2012, the coverage of cases with women as murder victims widened significantly, both in traditional (newspapers and television) and in new media channels (online journalism).[1] This new visibility lead to the development, by feminist activists and scholars, of a critique of the journalistic portrayal of femicide that can be labeled as metadiscourse, in light of its reflexive nature.

A crucial and precursory role, in this sense, was played by the media activist Luisa Betti, who denounced the frequent description of lethal gender violence cases as crimes of passion and outbursts of violence linked to jealousy or psychiatric issues (2014). According to Betti, this tendency, which is often coupled with the inclination to blame the victim for her behaviors, contributes to excuse the perpetrator, thus minimizing the social relevance of the phenomenon and its political implications (2014). Betti's insights on this topic were confirmed by a scholarly analysis published by Pina Lalli and Chiara Gius, which highlighted the frequent use of the frames of romantic love and loss of control in Italian news coverage (2014:63–66). The authors of the study contend that both frames present femicide as the "consequence of mere contingency" and, in so doing, validate "the idea that intimate partner femicides are not just impossible to prevent and to predict, but that they are part of the 'natural course of things.'" (71) Further research on the topic demonstrated the persistence of narrative techniques that absolve the perpetrator of responsibility (Abis and Orrù 2016; Giomi 2015:567–568) and objectify the victim by eroticizing her or by presenting her as subaltern to the partner/former partner (Abis and Orrù 2016).

DOI: 10.4324/9781003120339-1

Furthermore, the association of women journalists Gi.U.Li.A. (*Giornaliste Unite, Libere, Autonome*) [United, Free and Autonomous Women Journalists] provided the feminist metadiscourse on the representation of femicide in Italian media with a substantial contribution by disseminating the aforementioned insights and research among professionals and the general public. Among other activities, Gi.U.Li.A. translated and promoted the Guidelines for Reporting on Violence Against Women drafted by the International Federation of Journalists (IFJ) in 2014. The guidelines circulated widely among Italian journalists who participated in specific training courses organized by the association (Gaiaschi 2018:241). The document encourages reporters to use accurate, non-judgemental language that takes into account the victim's agency without blaming her. It also recommends journalists dealing with gender violence to make reference to the social context from which patriarchal abuse stems avoiding euphemistic, minimizing, and spectacularizing expressions (IFJ 2014).

This short outline testifies to the vitality of feminist discourse on femicide in Italy and shades light on the relevance of the metadiscourse on the portrayal of the phenomenon by media. Feminists' decision to embed in their critique of lethal gender violence a careful analysis of its representation demonstrates, in turn, the importance that narratives play in challenging the existing patriarchal *milieu* linked to the practice of gendered killing. In light of this, the present part investigates the reception of feminist theorizations on femicide and its portrayal in journalistic inquiries published in books, with the objective of evaluating the narratives' ability to engage ethically with femicidal events.

Investigative journalism on *Femminicidio*: general tendencies

Despite scholars having long discussed the lack of dynamism that seems to characterize investigative journalism in Italy (Pansa 1985; Bianda 2003; Bellu 2005; Agostini 2005), in the case of femicide this genre happens to be prolific and has produced a significant amount of books[2] and TV programs[3] but only a few in-depth investigations published in newspapers or magazines.[4] This is not surprising if we consider the general reluctance of Italian inquiries to occupy spaces traditionally associated with the journalistic practice and its corresponding tendency to expand into different channels (Bianda 2003; Bellu 2005; Agostini 2005). As Angelo Agostini pointed out, the Italian *inchiesta* has extensively permeated the non-fiction publishing sector (labeled as *saggistica* in the peninsula) to the point of revitalizing the book format

(2005:138). Among other things, this has been made possible by the increasing levels of integration between investigative journalism and feature writing, which resulted in the adoption of a narrative style that guarantees accessibility among a wide range of readers (Bianda 2006:198). For this reason, the genre of journalistic inquiry seems to fulfill the political function of building community and aggregation upon the discussion of social phenomena that affect the country, despite its chronic inability to directly affect Italian institutional power dynamics (Bianda 2006:199).

The associative and relational value of the inquiry is crucial to the narration of femicide because it allows the representation of gender-based violence as a systemic practice that involves all members of the community on different levels. To put it in other words, the inquiry is a genre that incentives people's aggregation and in so doing, serves the needs of feminist discourse, which insists on the importance of looking at femicide as the extreme manifestation of a continuum of violence embedded in the patriarchal culture that pervades all of society (Radford 1992:3–4). The relevance of such a narrative practice to the topic of lethal gender violence is confirmed by the success of the previously mentioned TV show format, which shares characteristics with journalistic inquiries published as books. As Enrico Bianda stressed, they both expand the space of the newspaper article into a broader piece where cases can be analyzed in-depth and they open up to the possibility of experimenting with narrative strategies explicitly aimed at triggering the emotional reaction of the reader/audience (2006:198).

Scholarly research on the representation of femicide in Italian TV programs dedicated to the in-depth coverage of the phenomenon has highlighted the emotional and empathic potential of the format (Binik 2015). However, the same programs have been extensively condemned by feminist critics who have noticed how they tend to build audience aggregation and sentimental participation on the basis of simplification and entertainment. Examples of this include the image of victims and perpetrators offered in TV shows like *Quarto grado* and *Amore criminale*, where murdered women are often depicted as ideal martyrs who conform to traditional gender roles (Binik 2015) while offenders are generally treated as people who kill out of deviancy or passion (Serra 2014). Together with these simplified representations that do not showcase the complexity of gender violence and its connection to the performance of patriarchal gender roles, TV programs such as *Amore criminale* present their narration as objective even when they mix factual and fictional elements (Serra 2014). As the president of the commission against femicide, Francesca Pugliesi, argued in a statement in which she asked for the withdrawal of the show from public television, this process of covered novelization exemplifies the sacrifice of gender violence's reality to entertainment purposes (*Repubblica* 2018).

Journalistic inquiries published as books, on the other hand, propose a more variegated set of narratives on the topic of lethal gender violence. As this selection aims to demonstrate, the potentials of the genre discussed above are exploited by some of the journalists who have decided to work on the issue, either by covering a specific story of femicide or by looking at the phenomenon from a broader perspective. The entertaining component is no stranger to inquiries published in books. In fact, these cultural products are influenced by the tendency that the Italian Media Studies scholar Milly Buonanno defined as *faction*, which describes the growing interest of journalistic texts to welcome fictional modes and intensely emotional registers within a factual narrative (1999:58–62).

Nevertheless, journalists who experiment with the written format seem to retain a deeper connection to the principle of counter-information [*controinformazione*]. Historically associated with the vast range of independent inquiries that blossomed in Italy during the highly politicized decades of the 1960s and the 1970s (Veneziani 2006:19–21), *controinformazione* refers to the practice of renarrating events that were previously simplified, concealed, or silenced by official media. In this sense, printed journalistic inquiries on femicide tend to present themselves as alternatives to the sensational and stereotypical representation of the phenomenon offered by periodical journalism and TV shows.

Moreover, printed investigative journalism showcases a relationship with the idea of authorship that differs from that displayed in newspaper articles or televised inquiries. The name of the journalist(s) who conducted the research always accompanies the text and the reference to the subjective dimension of the account plays a substantial role, to the point that some reporters make their subjective filter visible by means of implicit allusions to their positioning or through an introduction that clearly states the perspective from which the narration is built. This particular feature is crucial to the representation of nonfictional femicide cases because it guarantees a much more transparent and sincere connection to the reality of the phenomenon and to its related experiences. The specific consideration that investigative journalism demonstrates for the issue of authoriality testifies to the interconnections between the genre and literary writing. This is not a coincidence if we think that for a long time in southern European countries like Italy, journalism was "an extension of the worlds of literature and politics," which only started to have an autonomous status and an independent professional path at the end of the nineteenth century (Hallin and Mancini 2004:110).

The contamination with literary strategies such as subjective narration can also be associated with the tradition of the so-called *reportage narrativo* [narrative reportage], a hybrid journalistic sub-genre linked to the practice of travel writing whose origins can be traced back to the context of eighteenth and nineteenth century Europe, when it flourished as an output of the Grand Tour. In Italy, the *reportage narrativo* was popularized at the beginning of the twentieth century, with the introduction of the so-called *terza pagina* [third page], a section that Italian newspapers dedicated to cultural topics (Zangrandi 2003:9–10). Since then, the sub-genre has been exploited by a significant number of Italian authors, mainly literary writers who have decided to engage in the production of nonfictional texts (Papuzzi 1998:53–75; Zangrandi 2003:69–165; Bertoni 2009:28). The *reportage narrativo* predates Tom Wolfe's New Journalism, which was initiated during the 1960s in the United States and anticipates its tendency to adopt explicitly subjective narrative strategies as well as to reject the category of objectivity as an axle for the reporting process.

However, the influence exercised on the texts considered in this section by the *reportage narrativo* and by the New Journalism does not prevent the authors from retaining a specific interest in the ideas of documentable reality and truth. This particular tendency differentiates investigative journalism from the literary works that will be analyzed in the chapters included in the second part, which (mostly) engage with the portrayal of actual events but do not aim at offering a detailed account of the facts they represent and showcase a less linear relationship with the principle of truth.

The texts selected for analysis are the following: *Il sangue delle donne. Cronache di femminicidi in Umbria* [Women's Blood. Reports on Femicides in Umbria] (2014) by Alvaro Fiorucci, *Se questi sono gli uomini* [If These Are the Men] (2012) by Riccardo Iacona, and *Quello che resta – Storia di Stefania Noce, il femminicidio e i diritti delle donne nell'Italia d'oggi* [What Remains – The Story of Stefania Noce, Femicide, and Women's Rights in Italy Today] (2013) by Serena Maiorana. The order in which the texts are discussed is not chronological. On the contrary, it serves the analysis as it helps to categorize the works according to their degree of proximity to the style and ethos of periodical journalism. Although the study focuses on a limited number of books, it can shed light on the tendencies that dominate printed investigative journalism on femicide as well as on the discrepancies that characterize the genre.

Notes

1 A study carried out by Elisa Giomi demonstrates how in 2013 the number of newspaper articles dedicated to femicide cases multiplied and reached the national average of one piece per victim (2015:569).
2 Among these, *La scelta di Lea* (2013) by Marika Demaria, *L'amore criminale* (2014) by Matilde D'Errico, *Le amiche che non ho più* (2016) by Francesca Carollo, *I labirinti del male* (2013) by Rossella Diaz and Luciano Garofano, *Mia per sempre* (2013) by Cinzia Tani, and *Il sangue rosa* (2014) by Francesca Porco.
3 The previously mentioned *Amore criminale*, for example, is entirely dedicated to denouncing cases of intimate partner femicide. Produced by the national public television broadcaster RAI and aired weekly since 2007, the program consists of dramatized re-enactments of true femicide stories. *In quanto donne. Storie di ordinaria violenza* is a series of five documentaries centered on femicide televised in November 2018 by the entertainment broadcaster Real Time. Other TV shows such as *Quarto grado* (Mediaset) and *Chi l'ha visto* (RAI) often cover cases of lethal violence against women.
4 Journalistic inquiries on femicide in newspapers or magazines include articles (Gonnelli 2016; Lania 2016; Obber 2016) published in *Il corpo del delitto* (Rangeri, Di Genova and Pigliaru), a special issue of the newspaper *Il Manifesto*, and a few pieces proposed by the weekly magazine *L'Espresso* where perpetrators are interviewed (Testi 2019) and statistics on femicide are showcased (Torlone 2017).

Works cited

Abis, S. and Orrù, P. (2016) "Il femminicidio nella stampa italiana: un'indagine linguistica," *Gender/sexuality/italy* 3: https://www.gendersexualityitaly.com/wp-content/uploads/2016/12/2.-Orru%CC%80-and-Abis.pdf. Accessed 2 January 2021.

Agostini, A. (2005) "Si fanno poche inchieste? Oppure le inchieste contano poco?" *Problemi dell'informazione* 30(2):135–140.

Bellu, G. M. (2005) "Il giornalismo investigativo e l'etica pubblica," *Problemi dell'informazione* 30(2):141–145.

Bertoni, C. (2009). *Letteratura. e giornalismo*. Rome: Carocci.

Betti, L. (2014) "Femminicidio: per un'informazione che superi la rivittimizzazione mediatica," *M@gm@* 12(1): http://www.magma.analisiqualitativa.com/1201/articolo_10.htm. Accessed 3 January 2021.

Bianda, E. (2006) "Inchiesta giornalistica e opinione pubblica. Opacità e narrazione: chi vede chi?" *Problemi dell'informazione* 31(2):197–205.

Bianda, E. (2003) "Verso un ritorno del giornalismo d'approfondimento," in Sorrentino, C. (ed.), *Il giornalismo in Italia. Aspetti, processi produttivi, tendenze*. Rome: Carocci, pp. 245–259.

Binik, O. (2015) "Ideali e meritevoli: le donne vittime di femicidio nel dibattito pubblico in Italia. Uno studio sulla trasmissione *Quarto Grado*," *Studi culturali* 3:391–412.

Buonanno, M. (1999) *Faction. Soggetti mobili e generi ibridi nel giornalismo italiano degli anni novanta*. Naples: Liguori.

Carollo, F. (2016) *Le amiche che non ho più. Lucia, Federica, Roberta*. Naples: Tullio Pironti.

Demaria, M. (2013) *La scelta di Lea. La ribellione di una donna della 'ndrangheta*. Milan: Melampo.

D'Errico, M. (2014) *L'amore criminale*. Turin: Einaudi.

Diaz, R. and Garofano, L. (2013). *I labirinti del male. Femminicidio, stalking e violenza sulle donne: che cosa sono, come difendersi*. Formigine: Infinito Edizioni.

Gaiaschi, C. (2018) "Cambiare il giornalismo in ottica di genere. Il contributo di Gi.U.Li.A tra istituzioni e movimenti." in Bettaglio, M. Mandolini, N. and Ross, S. (eds.), *Rappresentare la violenza di genere. Sguardi femministi tra critica, attivismo e scrittura*. Milan: Mimesis, pp. 237–248

Giomi, E. (2015) "Tag femminicidio. La violenza letale contro le donne nella stampa italiana," *Problemi dell'informazione* 50(3):549–574.

Gius, C. and Lalli, P. (2014) "'I Loved Her So Much, but I Killed Her.' Romantic Love as a Representational Frame for Intimate Partner Femicide in Three Italian Newspapers," *Journal for Communication Studies* 7(2):53–75.

Gonnelli, R. (2016) "Una tovaglia fantasia 'cucita' regione per regione," in Rangeri, N., Di Genova, A., and Pigliaru, A. (ed.), *Il corpo del delitto, Il Manifesto*, pp. 8–10.

Hallin, D. and Mancini, P. (2004) *Comparing Media Systems. Three Models of Media and Politics*. Cambridge: Cambridge University Press.

IFJ. (2014) IFJ Guidelines for Reporting on Violence Against Women. *IFJ*. January 31: https://www.ifj.org/media-centre/news/detail/category/gender-equality/article/ifj-guidelines-for-reporting-on-violence-against-women-in-english-french-and-spanish.html. Accessed 3 January 2021.

Lania, C. (2016) "Schiave di 'Italo'. Comprate per il nostro sesso," in Rangeri, N., Di Genova, A., and Pigliaru, A. (eds.), *Il corpo del delitto, Il Manifesto*, pp. 16–17.

Obber, C. (2016) "Non lo faccio più. Una rabbia tutta da rieducare," in Di Genova, A., Rangeri, N., and Pigliaru, A. (eds.), *Il corpo del delitto, Il Manifesto*, pp. 53–54.

Pansa, G. (1985) "Si fanno poche inchieste: ecco cinque ragioni," *Problemi dell'informazione* 10(3):403–411.

Papuzzi, A. (1998) *Letteratura e giornalismo*. Rome-Bari: Laterza.

Porco, F. (2014) *Il sangue rosa. La strage delle donne*. Cosenza: Luigi Pellegrini Editore.

Radford, J. (1992) "Introduction," in Radford, J. and Russell, D. E. H. (eds.), *Femicide. The Politics of Women Killing*. New York: Twayne Publishers, pp. 3–12.

Rangeri, N., Di Genova, A. and Pigliaru, A. (eds.) (2016) Il corpo del delitto. *Il Manifesto*. November 9.

Repubblica. (2018) 'Amore criminale', commissione su femminicidio chiede chiusura del programma. January 15: https://www.repubblica.it/spettacoli/

tv-radio/2018/01/15/news/commissione_su_femminicidio_chiede_alla_rai_di_chiudere_di_amore_criminale_-186531516/. Accessed 10 January 2021.

Serra, P. (2014) Femminicidio: I pericolosi effetti del programma 'Amore Criminale' di RAI 3. *State of Mind.* December 2: https://www.stateofmind.it/2014/12/femminicidio-amore-criminale-rai3/. Accessed 10 January 2021.

Tani, C. (2013) *Mia per sempre. Quando lui la uccide per rabbia, vendetta, gelosia.* Milan: Mondadori.

Testi, E. (2019) Chi sono gli uomini che picchiano le donne. *L'Espresso.* March 8: http://espresso.repubblica.it/attualita/2019/03/07/news/chi-sono-gli-uomini-che-picchiano-le-donne-1.332439. Accessed 6 January 2021.

Torlone, G. (2017) Ogni due giorni una donna viene uccisa dal compagno. I numeri della violenza di genere. *L'Espresso.* June 21: http://espresso.repubblica.it/attualita/2017/06/19/news/femminicidi-1.304466. Accessed 4 January 2021.

Veneziani, M. (2006) *Controinformazione: stampa alternativa e giornalismo d'inchiesta dagli anni Sessanta a oggi.* Rome: Castelvecchi.

Zangrandi, S. (2003) *A servizio della realtà. Il reportage narrativo dalla Fallaci a Severgnini.* Milan: Unicopli.

2 *Il sangue delle donne* (2014) by Alvaro Fiorucci

Published in 2014, when the debate on femicide was already well underway, *Il sangue delle donne. Cronache di femminicidi in Umbria* is a collection of 64 accounts of murder cases in which the victim of violence is a woman or a girl. Its author, Alvaro Fiorucci, is a renowned journalist in Umbria, where he often collaborates with the local University Press, Morlacchi.[1] The regional outlook that characterizes *Il sangue delle donne* – all the murder cases collected in the book took place in the region – does not compromise its inclusion within the Italian general discourse on femicide, especially considering Umbria's nation-wide reputation for true crime-related narratives.[2]

Fiorucci's work opens with an introduction that provides the reader with a detailed summary of the common characteristics identified in the femicide cases, which refers back to the theoretical efforts undertaken by scholars who started employing the term femicide in order to describe the specific experience of women's victimization. The influence of feminist discourse on *Il sangue delle donne* is further demonstrated by the presence of constant allusions to the aforementioned metadiscourse on the representation of lethal gender violence and by its criticism of the portrayal offered by periodical journalism of femicides as extemporaneous episodes of outburst. It is no coincidence that Fiorucci quotes and labels as misleading the expressions "raptus, impeto, omicidio a caldo" [burst, impetus, sudden murder] (2014:9) that reporters frequently employ in the coverage of the most common form of femicide, intimate partner killings.[3] Conversely, the author insists on the idea of premeditation supported by a long-standing cultural attitude toward women's objectification and possession (9–11), which supports feminist theories in demystifying the phenomenon and describing it as a manifestation of the patriarchal symbolic order.

However, the constant implicit reference to the discourse and metadiscourse does not prevent the author from relying on the category

DOI: 10.4324/9781003120339-2

of sex, as opposed to the category of gender, to describe the social hierarchy that results in abusive behaviors. This inclination is expressed by the declared preference over the sex-based linguistic opposition male/female [*maschio/femmina*], instead of the gender-related man/woman [*uomo/donna*], which leads, unsurprisingly, to the depiction of femicide as an ancestral phenomenon linked to the supposed essential dimension of the relationship between the sexes:

> More than arithmetic this is algebra: the male wants to dispose of the female as he pleases. There is love, there is no love, this is a side matter. What counts is the sex and the roles. Male and female. As opposed to man and woman. Because the primordial bestiality that recurs when the first loses control over the second needs to be taken into account. (10)

In a similar fashion, Fiorucci's introduction discloses its tendency to draw on the stereotypical idea of women's fragility and passivity by labeling the femicide victim as a "weak subject." (10) The generally contradictory approach that characterizes the text epitomizes one of the effects of the mainstreaming of feminist discourse on femicide: the adoption of elements of feminist theorizations that criticize the most explicit manifestations of sexist domination and the rejection of those that radically contest the general patriarchal order. In this way, narratives like Fiorucci's align with a feminist perspective only on a superficial level, while continuing to convey problematic ideas and stereotypical constructions that are detrimental to the cultural struggle against femicide.

In the case of *Il sangue delle donne*, moreover, the effects of the hackneyed portrayal of lethal gender violence are amplified by the author's claim to provide an objective narration. The preface showcases the journalist's choice not to offer information about his positioning and, despite the presence of a conclusive signature (13), a subjective narration conveyed by the use of the first-person pronouns is clearly avoided. The lack of allusions to the authorial process contributes to the general appearance of the text as transparent and objective. This pretense is furtherly expressed by the frequent reference to the notion of *cronache*, an expression that does not have a precise English equivalent. The idea of *cronache* identifies narratives that retain an implicit vocation to neutrality or, to put it in Fiorucci's own words, reports that "never lie." (9) Although not revealed, the subjective filter is strongly present in *Il sangue delle donne* and it affects the author's stylistic choices, which often result in the adoption of narrative techniques that display a significant degree of fictionalization, as the analysis of the text will demonstrate in the following pages.

The supposed impartiality that the author associates to his journalistic practice is problematic for the representation of femicide-related events because it conceals the inevitable reshaping that the authorial voice forces into the process of victimization of women who cannot express themselves anymore. The tendency to obliterate the subjective dimension of the narrative is even more problematic in texts offering a highly stereotypical representation of the victims and the phenomenon, as is the case with Fiorucci. In fact, prejudicial thoughts and sexist categorizations stabilize in the reader's mind when the patina of objectivity is employed because every time the stereotype is exhibited as irrefutable product of reality (or of nature) it is confirmed within the current cultural order (Bourdieu 2002:11–12).

The critical aspects observed in the introduction reflect on the work's general structure, especially on the incoherencies that characterize the femicide stories covered, both in terms of typology and dedicated space. First of all, not all the crimes included in the book are classifiable as femicides, mainly because some of them are not a manifestation of gender violence. These include the murder of a landlady carried out by tenants who did not want to pay the rent, or the killing of two women clerks who were shot by a man who had lost his job. Far from being simple inaccuracies, these inclusions can be referred back to the aforementioned preference for the category of sex as opposed to that of gender. As an outcome, femicide is portrayed here as an event linked to the victim's sexual identity, not as the result of a specific gender-related motive legitimized by patriarchal culture.

Furthermore, the author demonstrates an inclination toward the narration of a victim typology that respects the stereotypical image of the local, white, and exemplary woman. Notwithstanding the laudable choice of covering cases where victims were prostitutes, migrants, and drug-addicts, these femicides only account for a maximum of two pages each, while those with "respectable" victims occupy up to a maximum of 23 pages. This disproportion mirrors the newsworthiness criteria identified in the analysis of periodical journalism on gender violence in Italy and beyond, where cases with native, young, attractive, and idealized women get more coverage (Christie 1986; Greer 2007:49; Giomi 2013:136–140). Reproducing the contradictory movement that we have already observed, the narrative practice negates the explicit criticisms that the author makes of periodical journalism's lack of interest for cases that are not particularly appealing or entertaining (Fiorucci 2014:209).

Moving from general observations on the structure to a detailed reading of the content and style of the text, it is clear that *Il sangue delle donne* follows personal reflections and uses narrative features borrowed from literary writing. These are often combined with excerpts from police or legal statements. If the personalisms and the emphatic tones remain disguised by the report's declared objectivity, the sources that Fiorucci quotes in his text are not always explicitly named and they are made recognizable as citations only by the presence of graphic peculiarities such as an indentation or the font size. The adoption of this technique provides the reader with a linear and unproblematized narrative, which is almost never interrupted, if not in the rare cases when the narrator comments on the official version of the story and, in challenging it, expresses the counter-informative approach that characterizes the work. Notwithstanding the presence of parts where the journalist criticizes the legal accounts, the author always chose to do so without exposing himself and by avoiding the use of first-person pronouns. In the following passage, for example, Fiorucci denounces a court sentence that insists on the absence of premeditation:

> During the Assize Court trial the pizzaiolo was condemned to 14 years in jail. […] The appeals process then established that the punishment for the author of a homicide that is not voluntary anymore, but negligent instead, is 11 years. Therefore, a homicide happened, but the killer did not want to kill. This is the judicial truth. Which is the only one that should be valid for everybody. (42)

Fiorucci adopts a clearly sarcastic tone here to contest the flaws of the official tale proposed during the trial, which he portrays as unreliable. This is suggested by his use of the temporal adverb "anymore" (*più*, in Italian), which evokes the inconsistency between the sentence expressed in the two degrees of judgment, as well as by the relativization of the word "truth," which is eloquently undermined by the juxtaposition to the adjective "judicial." The representation of the legal narrative as incomplete reads like an invitation to avoid producing accounts that are presented as universally valid, a task that Fiorucci himself fails to accomplish by neglecting to present his own narration as not being objective.

Both the criticism of the legal reports and the adoption of literary emphasis are used in *Il sangue delle donne* in order to sustain a victim-centered perspective that assigns relevance to the woman's experience of abuse. In parallel, they are employed to denounce the perpetrator's guilt and brutality, which results in a clear-cut depiction of the social hierarchy that manifests itself in the act(s) of violence. Fiorucci does not refrain from the use of an esthetically vigilant style and includes in its writing creative (or fictional) elements, such as references to the victims' feelings, which cannot be verified as they were presumably experienced by a dead woman. An example is the text "Mamma ti voglio bene" [Mum, I love you], where the journalist tells the story of a woman being murdered by her son:

> She feels the blade entering and retracting from her back, four times. Two energetic and violent slashes, from top to bottom, because she is leaning on the sink and he is taller than her. She feels the pain blocking her breath. She feels the blood gushing with force from her body until she ends up against the wall, next to the stove where she just prepared coffee. She turns, but on her face there is no anguish, there is surprise, incredulity. To the person in front of her she would like to ask: "Why?" […] He will not be prosecuted, he will be cured. He will manage to climb out of the black wheel where, while falling, he dragged with him his mother, who that day wanted to tell him with a caress how big her love for him was. (105–106)

The process of fictionalization through which Fiorucci ascribes thoughts and feelings to the femicide victim clearly serves a stereotypical representation of the woman, who is depicted as the perfect loving mother and, consequently, fits into the prototype of the ideal victim. This is not surprising if we consider that the construction of stereotypes is usually linked to the need of compensating the lack of direct experience with generic observations or opinions derived from an imaginary practice that relies on common-sense or hearsay (Lippmann 1991:79–80). To put that in other words, the mechanisms of fictional representation conceptually overlap with those that pertain to the development of prejudicial thought, which proves fictionalization to be a delicate practice for feminist portrayals of femicide.

On a similar note, Fiorucci employs fictional narrative devices to emphasize the description of the perpetrator, as demonstrated by the following excerpt:

> The dark man arrives when it's dark. It is almost 8 PM on 16 November 2006 and on the stairs of the apartment building at 45 Purgotti Street, Perugia, there is not enough light. The dark man

> moves, determined. He enters and leaves the apartment belonging to Sonia Marra, a 25 year old from Specchia, Lecce, who came to Perugia to study to become a biomedical technician. A girl notices him [...] He wears a black coat with a hood. His body is monumental. He truly resembles the dark man of storytelling and horror movies. Sonia has not picked up the phone for hours. And she will not pick it up anymore. (161)

The portrayal of the unknown killer as the dark man, the frightening and dangerous figure of childhood mythology seen through the eyes of a little girl, strengthens the stereotypical idea of the femicide author as the embodiment of alterity. This idea is further backed by the reference to the horror narrative genre that, in its canonical form, uses the category of the monstrous in order to exclude the murderer from the sphere of normativity. If, as the philosopher Paul Santilli puts it, horror is "the shock of that which cannot even be defined or located in a spectrum of values," (2007:178–179) the representation of femicide as a horrific event fails to recognize the phenomenon's actual dependency to the set of principles promoted by patriarchal culture.

Fictionalization is not the only literary technique employed in the aforementioned excerpts. Suspense narrative is another, and it can be observed in the construction of the text as a build-up of details that lead to the climax of the victim's death or disappearance. As the narratologist Noël Carroll stressed, the main characteristic of suspense narratives is their focus on a feeling of uncertainty that leaves room for the actualization of only one out of two opposite possibilities, which are respectively symbolized as moral and immoral. This unpredictability maintains the spectator/reader's interest until the realization of one alternative or the other (Carroll 1990:137). In light of this, suspense can be read as a narrative device that engages the reader on the basis of a Manichean distinction between good and evil. This is why, when it comes to femicide coverage, suspense is often linked to the polarizing representations of the victim and the perpetrator as incarnations respectively of supreme morality and immorality.

The reduction of lethal gender violence to this dualism aligns with feminist metadiscourse on the portrayal of femicide, according to which the actual hierarchy of violence needs to be stated in order to reverse misleading representations that blame the victim or excuse the perpetrator. However, the insistence on such an opposition risks to reinforce rather than challenge an essentialist depiction of the phenomenon, as it is based on the same dichotomous logic that sustains the patriarchal symbolic order that legitimizes gendered domination and violence (Bourdieu 2002:12–14). In the first extract from *Il sangue delle donne*, for example, suspense contributes to the stereotypical opposition between the good loving mother (the victim) and the disturbing figure of the crazy son (the perpetrator) who embodies the alterity of evil. In the second excerpt, the tension builds on the representation of the killer as a deviant and monstrous figure in opposition to the human and normal woman victim.

As we have seen in Fiorucci's work, literary style acts as a channel for the popularization of feminist rhetoric on issues such as the representation of the distinction between victim and perpetrator, but it ends up trapping it in a rigid dichotomy that betrays the feminist ethos itself. In other parts of the text, *faction* also contributes to reinforcing sexist prejudices like that of the objectified woman, as do narrative procedures such as the spectacularization of femicide. This tendency is exemplified by the title of the book, which employs an emphatic tone and relies on references to the highly spectacular symbolism of the blood that can easily be linked to essentialist stances. In the rest of the work, there are frequent instances of passages where literary style and suspense techniques are associated with the reification and erotization of the dead women's bodies. In the following extract, for example, the victim's physical dimension is deconstructed and reduced to a series of separated entities that are often connoted in sexual terms. The artfully orchestrated tension discloses an image in which the woman's personal integrity is completely dismembered:

> It only takes a few moments for the two guys to focus (on) the scene. Here are the legs. Those are the leggings that covered just the knees. That is the chest covered by a white t-shirt which is so wrinkled that it is rolled-up at the level of the breasts. That is the face, with the eyes, and short hair on the forehead. The back of the head is wounded and the bruising is evident. They are observing a corpse. (Fiorucci 2014:247)

Moreover, it is through the use of factional narrative modes that the author misrepresents the femicidal behavior as dependent on mysterious and alien forces that are exogenous to the realm of patriarchal normativity. In the first of the long series of accounts provided in the book, Fiorucci reiterates the association between the perpetrator – a father who abuses his young daughter while participating in séances – and malicious entities. He is described as a satanic individual, as the frequent use of metaphors linked to the isotopy of the diabolic testify: "She lives in contact with the 'Devil'";

(19) "The prosecution talks about rape and indecent exposure to minor. At least four years lived as if in hell"; (25) "Before her eyes she has the image of Satan." (34)

Notwithstanding the adoption of narrative elements taken from the literary tradition, *Il sangue delle donne* does not comply with the textual typology that Iser (1972) defines as productive for the promotion of the reader's identification. Instead of allowing fruitful space for the reader's interpretation, Fiorucci replaces the interpretative margins that the police and legal documents leave uncovered through a narrative that turns to the products of journalistic investigation or to the aforementioned practice of fictionalization. If omissions are rare in the text, other techniques that could stimulate a participatory reading are also missing, due to the lack of a positioned narration that prevents the author from constructing an intersubjective dimension in which the receiver's feelings and behaviors could be mirrored. The text's inability to engage the reader in an identification process is a critical aspect in the representation of femicide because it inhibits the possibility of a profound and personal comprehension of the pervasive dynamics that lead to the act of sexist violence.

To conclude, *Il sangue delle donne* reproduces most of the problematic tendencies identified by Italian feminists in the coverage of lethal gender violence. In fact, notwithstanding the declared intention to act as a counter-informative text, Fiorucci's work relies on a supposedly objective narration that superficially follows the directions of feminist metadiscourse on femicide, while on a deeper level it supports a stereotypical depiction of the phenomenon.

Notes

1 He published three other investigative texts with the press: *Il cacciatore di bambini. Biografia non autorizzata del mostro di Foligno* (2013), *48 small. Il dottore di Perugia e il mostro di Firenze* (2012) and he co-authored with Raffaele Guadagno *Il divo e il giornalista. Giulio Andreotti e l'omicidio di Carmine Pecorelli: frammenti di un processo dimenticato* (2017).

2 Umbria was in the spotlight of Italian journalists for at least two major cases happened during the Nineties and the first decade of the new century: the case of a serial murderer labeled as *mostro di Foligno* [The Monster of Foligno], who killed two boys in a provincial town of the region between 1992 and 1993, and the unsolved killing of the British student Meredith Kercher, which happened in Perugia in November 2007.

3 All translations from Italian, unless otherwise stated, are mine.

Works cited

Bourdieu, P. (2002) [1998] *Masculine Domination.* Tran. R. Nice. Bloomington: Stanford University Press.

Carroll, N. (1990) *The Philosophy of Horror or Paradoxes of the Heart.* New York and London: Routledge.

Christie, N. (1986) "The Ideal Victim," in Fattaj, E. A. (ed.), *From Crime Policy to Victim Policy. Reorienting the Justice System.* New York: Palgrave, pp. 17–30.

Fiorucci, A. (2012) *48 small. Il dottore di Perugia e il mostro di Firenze.* Perugia: Morlacchi.

Fiorucci, A. (2013) *Il cacciatore di bambini. Biografia non autorizzata del mostro di Foligno.* Perugia: Morlacchi.

Fiorucci, A. (2014) *Il sangue delle donne.* Perugia: Morlacchi.

Fiorucci, A. and Guadagno, R. (2017) *Il divo e il giornalista, Giulio Andreotti e il caso Carmine Pecorelli: frammenti di un processo dimenticato.* Perugia: Morlacchi.

Giomi, E. (2013) "Il femminicidio nelle relazioni intime: analisi quantitative del fenomeno e della sua rappresentazione nei TG italiani," in Magaraggia, S. and Cherubini, D. (eds.), *Uomini che odiano le donne? Le radici della violenza maschile.* Turin: UTET, pp. 131–151.

Greer, C. (2007) "News Media, Victims and Crime," in Davies, P., Francis, P. and Greer, C. (eds.), *Victims, Crime and Society.* Los Angeles, London, New Delhi, Singapore: Sage, pp. 20–49.

Iser, W. (1972) "The Reading Process: A Phenomenological Approach," *New Literary History* 3(2):279–299.

Lippmann, W. (1991) [1922] *Public Opinion.* New Brunswick and London: Transaction Publishers.

Santilli, P. (2007) "Culture, Evil, and Horror," *The American Journal of Economics and Sociology* 66(1):173–194.

3 *Se questi sono gli uomini* (2012) by Riccardo Iacona

Written by the journalist Riccardo Iacona,[1] *Se questi sono gli uomini* came out in October 2012, at the end of the year that saw feminist discourse on lethal gender violence enter the mainstream. The publication of the book was followed by an episode of the RAI TV program *Presa Diretta* hosted by Iacona himself and entitled *Strage di donne* [Women's Massacre], which was broadcast on February 23, 2013.[2] This testifies to the work's wide circulation, which is further demonstrated by the presence of reviews in some major Italian newspapers, by the production of a short booktrailer for the education channel RAIScuola, and by the publisher's decision to reprint the book in 2015.

Iacona's work – both in its printed and televised format – follows the model of the traditional *reportage narrativo*. This is demonstrated by the explicit references to the travel dimension and to the subjective documentary vocation that are typical of the genre (Zangrandi 2003:10). In the preface to the text, for example, Iacona describes the inquiry on a few femicide cases that occurred in Italy in the spring of 2012 using these words: "The story you are about to read is the account of a few month's travel which started in Enna and ended in Milan." (2012b:3) The theme of the personal journey is retrieved and expanded within the following lines, to the point that the report of the trip from the South to the North of Italy ends up being presented as an exemplary manifestation of a collective story anchored in the social, cultural, and geographical *milieu* of the Italian peninsula: "This is a story that belongs to everybody, because it tells how we really are, nobody should feel excluded. This is an Italian story." (Iacona 2012b:4)

The allusion to a collective subjectivity conveyed by the use of the first-person pronoun "we" links the preface to the last section of the book entitled "Noi, gli uomini" [We, the men]. Written in collaboration with Giulia Bosetti, one of Iacona's fellow journalists in the TV

DOI: 10.4324/9781003120339-3

program *Presa Diretta*, this part includes testimonies of perpetrators collected in a rehabilitation center in Bozen. By interposing his personal authorial voice between the abusers' declarations and by situating himself as a subject who identifies with the male gender, Iacona explicitly addresses the readers and asks them to undertake a process of self-analysis through which they identify in their own behaviors the long series of abusive and controlling attitudes that are linked to the actual phenomenon of gender violence: "Now, if we want to understand how deep and rooted violence against women in our country is, as men – and I consider myself part of this category – we need to do a small exercise: how many of us do recognize ourselves in these stories, even if only in part?" (205) The stylistic choice of the direct question stimulates the receivers to recognize in the familiarity of their own actions the perturbing elements of the femicidal conduct. Therefore, it forces them to reveal their complicity with patriarchal domination. Iacona's operation can be described as a form of intersubjective dialog with the male readers that allows the reconstruction of the connection between the positioned authorial voice, the receivers, and the supposed alterity of the murderer/abuser. While doing so, the journalist dismantles the misleading idea that sexist violence is a form of deviancy from the category of hegemonic masculinity (Connell 2005).

The specificity of the reading response potentially activated by *Se questi sono gli uomini* – which will be labeled as mirroring from now on – does not correspond to the aforementioned identification process theorized by Iser (1972). If the Iserian identification describes a type of engagement with the narrative practice triggered by the presence of omissions that need to be filled by the reader, then mirroring corresponds to the empathetic association of the receiver with one or more characters. For Keith Oatley, mirroring happens when the reader and the character(s) have the same objectives or projects, or if they carry out the same sort of actions (1994:65). Similarly, Suzanne Keen argued that mirroring[3] results in the development of a fruitful empathy in the reader but it is usually associated with the common recognition of receiver and character(s) as part of the same identity categories (gender, age, race, etc.) or as driven by analogous aims (2006:2014). In light of this, mirroring is a productive but limited tool for the effective representation of lethal gender violence, because it does not guarantee readers' compassionate reactions to identity groups to which they do not belong. This is clearly demonstrated by Iacona's text that highlights the gendered dimension of the phenomenon by encouraging a feeling of affinity between men but, at the same time, risks to corroborate patriarchal dichotomies by building the mirroring process on the principle of gender partition.

If references to a collective subjectivity are placed at the beginning and at the end of the book to create a circular structure on the core theme of common introjection of patriarchal culture, the adoption of the first-person pronoun "I" characterizes the whole text. Iacona's choice to make extensive use of subjective narration testifies to the author's interest in presenting his work as a piece of journalistic documentation merged with the genre of personal testimony. The testimony dimension of the work is also conveyed by the title, which makes a clear allusion to Primo Levi's seminal work *Se questo è un uomo* [If This Is a Man] (1947). Levi's memoir on his experience of incarceration in Auschwitz is a cornerstone of the Italian literary tradition on testimonial auto/biography which, if read together with his collection of essays *I sommersi e i salvati* [The Drowned and the Saved] (1986), offers insights into the practice of witnessing and its ethical implications. The role assigned to testimony by Levi's reflection is problematic and crucial at the same time: on one side, testimony is always ambiguous because it depends on human memory, which is labeled at the beginning of the book as a "wonderful but fallacious instrument"; (Levi 1988:11) on the other, it is a practice that can provide a genuine, albeit subjective, and inevitably partial, account of the experience of violence suffered by the subject or by those who can no longer articulate their denunciation.

The authorial voice emerges clearly in the central sections of the inquiry, where Iacona comments on his encounters with friends and relatives of the victims and describes the places he visits during the journey. These reports often incorporate judicial documents, such as the transcription of the confession of the killer of a young Sicilian woman (Vanessa Scialfa) that opens the book, but they do not leave out observations and personal remarks. Examples include the impressions arising from the inspection in the apartment where one of the women was killed. Here the narrative style relies on the use of the isotopy of the dark to convey the writer's gloomy and compassionate feelings, which are clearly presented as the outcome of a subjective perception: "The first thing I notice are the closed blinds: that day they argued in the dark, I think"; (Iacona 2012b:44) "Before leaving the apartment, the police turned off all the lights and I stared for a bit more at the murder scene: a small studio in the dark, with a few pieces of furniture, a couple of stoves, a couch, a mattress, and a toilet. It is empty like a prison cell. Poor girl, who died in this place with no colors." (44–45)

Notwithstanding the reiteration of the role played by subjective mediation, *Se questi sono gli uomini* showcases a deep respect for the journalistic ethos, which results in the choice of adhering as much as possible to the facts that were witnessed or to the sources with which the author interacts. This approach is confirmed by the extensive presence of quotation marks used to delimit the witnesses' statements or to confirm the authenticity of narrative excerpts where the authorial filter is not explicitly declared. It is not a coincidence that Iacona's text tends to avoid fictionalization and does not lean on the practice of creative narrative in order to fill the gaps left by the documentation process. On the contrary, the journalist makes clear reference to his interest in collecting the "gleams of truth" (51) emerging from the action of digging beyond the surface of consolatory narratives that surround the femicidal events. To put it differently, in *Se questi sono gli uomini* the reporter's task coincides with sidestepping social censorships that conceal the tumultuous reality of human relationships by dredging up distressing "fractures of meaning," (51) with the general aim of remaining respectful toward the materiality of the phenomenon. For Iacona, there is no stainless truth to be elicited but only fragments of reality that need to be interrogated in the context of a positioned narrative that declares its partiality as well as its desire to reach the closest proximity to the real.

It is precisely on the aforementioned tendency of the investigative subject to observe what surrounds him with the objective of dismantling reassuring interpretations of the phenomenon that the counter-informative approach of Iacona's work is based. In particular, the author's intention to shape his inquiry on the deconstruction of periodical journalism's rhetoric on the topic is clear. The first two sections of the book ("Vanessa Scialfa" and "Rosa Trovato"), for example, contest the idea of femicide as resulting from of a sudden outburst or from the behavior of a mad or sick man. Following the recommendations of feminist metadiscourse on lethal gender violence, Iacona insists in reporting the details of police examinations from which the perpetrator's clarity of mind emerges. This is the case with Vanessa Scialfa's murderer, who is presented as an aware killer "who could have stopped at any time," even after the first eruption of anger (6). Iacona also denounces the propensity to consider femicide as a "bad business that does not concern us, because it cannot happen to us, being a set of stories that involve: 'mad people,' 'sick people,' 'poor people,' 'depressed areas.'" (50)

The aforementioned decision to rely on a discourse that recognizes the principle of exemplarity, as opposed to that of exceptionality, as key to interpreting gender-based violence, guides Iacona's critique of the polarization between the angelic victim and the ruthless perpetrator.

The opposition, which is recognized by Marian Meyers as a common feature in the newspaper coverage of femicide cases with brutally murdered young victims (1996:57–61), is explicitly condemned by the journalist, who labels it as product of a "TV show" rhetoric (16). The author challenges this discursive process of othering by instead promoting a portrayal of victims and perpetrators as common individuals who experience a relational breakdown that readers can potentially recognize as part of their life experience. In this regard, the portrayal of Vanessa Scialfa's killer, Francesco Lo Presti, whose possessive behavior is compared to that of the victim's previous partner, Alessandro, is emblematic. In his interview with Iacona, Alessandro reveals the same tendency to isolate and control the woman that the journalist's account had already identified in the description of Lo Presti's conduct as a legacy of Sicilian patriarchal society.

Furthermore, the pervasiveness of sexist culture is highlighted by the figure of Alessandro's mother, who, during the interview, justifies her son's dominating attitude saying: "He cares about the girl, and rightly so. [...] When Vanessa used to work the night shift at the bar, my son didn't sleep. He was always on his phone trying to call her. [...] Obviously, it is not right to disturb someone while she is working, but my son cared about Vanessa and this is why they used to argue. He was crazy about her." (10) By reporting the woman's defense of her son's conformity to the hegemonic masculinity model, Iacona introduces the reader to the eventuality of women's collusion with sexist attitudes and, in so doing, he troubles the linearity of the dichotomy male-perpetrator vs female-victim. This is particularly relevant if we consider that sociological research on behaviors supporting patriarchal ideology has demonstrated how the desire to maintain the current order and hierarchies is not strictly related to the gender identity of the subject (Sibley et al. 2007; Roets et al. 2012). As Roets et al. maintain, "in modern Western society, it is warranted to (also) consider sexism at the individual level in terms of differences in general motivated cognitive style and specific social attitudes, rather than merely in terms of a group phenomenon or a 'battle between the sexes.'" (2012:357)

As testified by these examples, the murderers in *Se questi sono gli uomini* are rarely presented as deviants or as monstrous creatures; on the contrary, the authors of femicide are treated as subjects who, like most men, benefit from the gender privilege allocated on the basis of the current social hierarchy. This gender privilege is realistically portrayed as an advantage that risks turning into an onerous burden whenever it develops into a personality trait that escalates into violence, as the following declaration by one of the abusive men interviewed in the book illustrates:

> Now I can understand a woman's point of view better. If you bang your fist on the table, it makes no difference to you, while for her, it is an act of bullying. You think that violence gives you power, but the truth is that violence is not power. First of all, it is a tool through which you hurt yourself. We are all victims, those who use violence are victims, perpetrators and victims at the same time. (Iacona 2012b:202)

The ability to recognize in his own attitude a manifestation of sexist arrogance, which the man has acquired during the reeducation process in the center where Iacona's collaborator carried out the interviews, goes hand in hand with the awareness of gendered psychosocial conditioning. In this specific case, he points the finger at the general tendency not to educate men to consider women's point of view, which derives from the patriarchal cultural construction of woman as man's Other. Or to rephrase, as the object of the male subject whose perspective is not worth acknowledging. The ex-abuser interprets his previous inability to recognize his partner's will as the origin of the violent action. But the abusive behavior does not support the man's personal integrity; on the contrary, it is seen as a tool that damages the subjectivity of both the victim and the perpetrator.

Following the insights offered by Jessica Benjamin, the man's statement can be read as the description of the dynamics that lead to the personal (as well as political) phenomenon of domination. Benjamin draws on the theories proposed by the father of relational psychoanalysis, Donald W. Winnicot, to explain how dominant behaviors could be traced back to the development phase where the child attempts at emancipating from the primary carer (usually the mother). If, as she maintains, the process of personal construction is always based on mutual recognition, when the child fails to perceive the (m) Other as a subject they become unable to build their own subjectivity. This process, which is supported by the patriarchal ideology of maternal nurturance as an act of totalizing dedication to the infant, results in a dangerous sentiment of dependency that progressively unfolds into a tendency to exert control on others. As Benjamin writes: "The self's aspiration to be absolute destroys the self, as well as the other, for as long as the other cannot face the self as an equal in the struggle, the battle results in loss and not mutual recognition." (1990:215) In light of this, the abusive man interviewed in Iacona's book highlights the dependency of femicidal behavior from societal prescriptions that preclude him, as well as the woman, from the possibility of an intersubjective relationality. For the same reasons, he labels himself as a victim of his own violence without relieving himself from the responsibility of being a perpetrator.[4]

When it comes to the representation of the victim, Iacona's narrative is not free from idealizations, but it turns out to be respectful enough of the women's heterogeneity and it demonstrates a constant attempt to overcome the limitations imposed by the gender cultural superstructure. In the opening case, the young Vanessa Scialfa is described as a responsible person with angelic features by the members of her family and friends (Iacona 2012b:12;15), thus reproducing the reassuring image of the ideal victim that characterizes the coverage of femicide in periodical journalism. However, from the second murder case onwards, the victims are portrayed as multifaceted individuals whose characteristics do not necessarily coincide with the stereotype of passive femininity. Rosa Trovato, for example, "is not that poor woman that people described, she is not a subjugated person who lives in a depressed environment. On the contrary, she is someone who stays out all day, who goes around on her motorbike, who takes care of her daughter in the morning as well as in the evening while maintaining the whole family with her job." (53) Instead of stigmatizing Rosa as a weak woman who did not find the courage to denounce her husband's violence, the journalist recognizes her as a strong individual who engages in activities that do not align with her gender role. Similarly, Eleonora Liberatore is presented as an independent woman who was murdered "in the place of her emancipation," "the factory where she worked." (132–133)

The portrayal of Stefania Garattoni, a twenty-year old killed by her ex-boyfriend Luca Lorenzoni, is also worth mentioning. Notwithstanding the women's young age and her fitting the profile for a representation as ideal victim, Iacona sketches a multidimensional portrait using the diary entries that Garattoni left as well as the statements that her sister gave to the police. By employing this technique, which allows the writer to minimize the risks of appropriating the story of her victimization to his own narrative, the journalist pictures Garattoni as a victim equipped with the clear ability to identify the boyfriend as her abuser. This is demonstrated by her decision to nickname him as Hannibal Lecter, the bloodthirsty protagonist of Tomas Harris' *The Silence of the Lambs* (1988), in her journal (145). Although she is aware of being a "test subject" (142) at the mercy of her boyfriend's desire for domination, Garattoni surrenders to all types of physical and psychological violence for five years, until she decides to walk away from the relationship and gets killed. The victim's perseverance in accepting a part in the sadistic game played by Lorenzoni does not result in the display of a judgmental attitude by the author, who, on the contrary, describes Gatattoni as a young woman whose "consciousness and lucidity were impressive," using the words of the vice-police administrator Silvia Gentilini (134).

As in the case of Rosa Trovato, Iacona's complex representation of Stefania Garattoni succeeds in challenging the common assumption that the victim of violence who endures constant oppression could be considered unaware or lacking in agency, thus contesting implicitly the oppositional logic upon which the patriarchal gendered order is built. The topic has been discussed extensively by Italian feminist activists, who have pointed out how the objectification established by the violent act should not be confirmed by a representational process that insists on the supposed passivity of the woman without recognizing the intricate web of emotional, social, or financial impediments that victims often face when it comes to actively confront abusive behaviors.[5]

In light of this analysis, it is clear that *Se questi sono gli uomini* encourages a revision of the patriarchal notion of femininity, which results in the decision not to reproduce the spectacularization of women's dead bodies. However, Iacona's insistence on the criticism of the cultural construction of gender does not go as far as making reference to victims who do not conform to the cis-gender model, which would have implicitly denied the dependence of femicide on the category of sex. In fact, the journalist's interest in providing an overview of power relationships within the heteronormative couple prevents him from including among the numerous cases analyzed the femicides of transgender women or nonbinary subjects. This absence is not compensated by a clear rejection of the gender dichotomy, which is described, analyzed, and even criticized in its stereotypical crystallization but does not undergo a radical process of discursive renewal that could lead to a fruitful deconstruction of the categories of masculinity and femininity.

Notes

1 Known to the wide public for *Presa diretta*, a TV program based on journalistic inquiries started in 2009, Iacona also published *Racconti d'Italia* (2007), *L'Italia in presadiretta* (2010), *Utilizzatori finali* (2014), and *Palazzo d'ingiustizia: il caso Robledo e l'indipendenza della magistratura* (2018).

2 The first part of the episode consists of the assembly of the footage collected during the same trip from which the book stems. The second half is dedicated to an inquiry on the work of Italian shelters for abused women.

3 Both Oatley and Keen reproduce the general tendency of Anglophone scholars of Reader Response Theory to use the term identification when talking about the process of emphatic mirroring. My preference for the term mirroring, as opposed to identification, relates to the need of providing the reader of this work with a clear distinction between the two practices.

4 On this declaration of guilt is based the difference between the ex-abuser's statement and what Michael Kimmel defined as "cultural construction of aggrieved entitlement." Kimmel's expression identifies the self-victimization performed by men and perpetrators who consider themselves disadvantaged because of the recent growth of movements and political practices that contest male privilege (2013:31–61;99–134). Notwithstanding this discrepancy, the overlapping of the categories of victim and perpetrator is a problematic rhetorical praxis as it runs the risk of supporting the aforementioned tendency of judicial and journalistic discourse to invert the actual hierarchy of gender violence by blaming the victim and excusing the perpetrator. In Iacona's case, however, the representation of a coexistence of the two categories in the abuser's persona offers a clear image of the social conditioning from which sexist violence stems.

5 In May 2015, for example, Italian activists and journalists launched the social media hashtag campaign #*Perchenonhodenunciato* [Why I did not denounce] where they invited other women to tell their story of abuse and explain publicly the variety of reasons that prevented them from issuing a complaint to the authorities. The stories highlighted the systemic dimension of gender violence, which can rarely be overcome with the mere act of denunciation and often leads to the judiciary, social or even physical re-victimization of the woman who decides to speak out. On this topic see Betti (2015), Gennaro (2015), Pronzato (2015).

Works cited

Benjamin, J. (1990) *The Bonds of Love. Psychoanalysis, Feminism, and the Problem of Domination*. London: Virago.

Betti, L. (2015) Tag: perché non ho denunciato. *DonnexDiritti*. May 29: https://donnexdiritti.com/tag/perche-non-ho-denunciato/. Accessed 27 July 2019.

Connell, R. (2005) [1995] *Masculinities*. Berkeley and Los Angeles: University of California Press.

Gennaro, A. (2015) Perché non ho denunciato. Il #DenimDay, una giornata per parlare, finamlmente. *Huffingtonpost*. May 29: https://www.huffingtonpost.it/angela-gennaro/perche-non-ho-denunciato-il-denimday-una-giornata-per-parlare-finalmente_b_7469272.html. Accessed 22 January 2021.

Iacona, R. (2007) *Racconti d'Italia*. Turin: Einaudi.

Iacona, R. (2012a) *L'Italia in presadiretta (Viaggio nel paese abbandonato dalla politica)*. Milan: Chiarelettere.

Iacona, R. (2012b) *Se questi sono gli uomini*. Milan: Chiarelettere.

Iacona, R. (2014) *Utilizzatori finali (Italia 2014. Sesso, festini hard, madri compiacenti e professionisti senza scrupoli)*. Milan: Chiarelettere.

Iacona, R. (2018) *Palazzo d'ingiustizia: il caso Robledo e l'indipendenza della magistratura*. Venice: Marsilio.

Iser, W. (1972) "The Reading Process: A Phenomenological Approach," *New Literary History* 3(2):279–299.

Keen, S. (2006) "A Theory of Narrative Empathy," *Narrative* 14(3):207–236.

Kimmel, M. (2013) *Angry White Men. American Masculinity and the End of an Era*. New York: Nation Books.

Levi, P. (1988) [1986] *The Drowned and the Saved.* Transl. Raymond Rosenthal. London: Michael Joseph.

Meyers, M. (1996) *News Coverage of Violence Against Women. Engendering Blame*. Thousand Oaks: Sage.

Oatley, K. (1994) "A Taxonomy of the Emotions of Literary Response and a Theory of Identification in Fictional Narrative," *Poetics* 23:53–74.

Pronzato, L. (2015) Perché non ho denunciato. *La 27esima ora*. May 29: https://27esimaora.corriere.it/articolo/perche-non-ho-denunciato/. Accessed 7 January 2021.

Roets, A., Van Hiel A. and Dhont, K. (2012) "Is Sexism a Gender Issue? A Motivated Social Cognition Perspective on Men's and Women's Sexist Attitudes Toward Own and Other Gender," *European Journal of Personality* 26(3):350–359.

Sibley, C. G., Overall, N. C. and Duckitt, J. (2007) "When Women Become More Hostilely Sexist toward Their Gender: The System-Justifying Effect of Benevolent Sexism," *Sex Roles* 57:743–754.

Zangrandi, S. (2003) *A servizio della realtà. Il reportage narrativo dalla Fallaci a Severgnini.* Milan: Unicopli.

4 *Quello che resta* (2013) by Serena Maiorana

The last work analyzed in this part, *Quello che resta: storia di Stefania Noce, il femminicidio e i diritti delle donne nell'Italia d'oggi* (2013) by the writer and young journalist Serena Maiorana, is a hybrid text that incorporates the genres of testimonial biography and journalistic inquiry. Despite its limited circulation, the text was warmly welcomed in cultural and feminist circles, where the author was frequently interviewed and invited for book launches. Moreover, the work received critical attention, being analyzed in a recent publication on the topic of gender-based violence and its representations in Italy (Pickering-Iazzi 2018).

As Robin Pickering-Iazzi noted, the author's choice to use statements of relatives and friends to recount the story of the feminist activist Stefania Noce, killed by her ex-partner in 2011, perfectly corresponds to the method adopted in testimonial biography (2018:82). The counter-informative style and the clear intention to provide the reader with a piece of feature writing on the topic of lethal gender violence in Italy, on the other hand, aligns with the genre of the inquiry.

The conformity of *Quello che resta* to the ethos of counter-information is clearly demonstrated in the second half of the book and, in particular, in a section entitled "Il linguaggio" [The language], where Maiorana openly criticizes mainstream journalism and its tendency to portray femicide resorting to tropes typically used in the romance novel, such as those of passion, jealousy, and romanticism (2013:30). In the same section, the writer makes explicit reference to the feminist metadiscourse on femicide and mentions campaigns launched by associations such as the aforementioned Gi.U.Li.A and *Un altro genere di comunicazione* (31).[1] Moreover, an allusion to the journalistic coverage is present in a chapter dedicated to the decision to condemn the killer, Loris Gagliano, to a life sentence for premeditated

DOI: 10.4324/9781003120339-4

murder. Maiorana blames the use of the expression *raptus di gelosia* [fit of jealousy] employed by the press despite the fact that the man's intention to kill was clearly highlighted in court (51), which confirms the general propensity to label lethal gender violence as an eruption of passion identified by scholars in Italian newspaper reports on femicide up until 2012 (Giomi 2010; Gius and Lalli 2014).

The purpose of developing a narrative that refutes dominant representative patterns is affirmed, though in an implicit manner, from the very beginning of the biography, given the writer's declared commitment to avoid a sensationalistic approach and to comply with a journalistic ethos that prevents her from circulating misleading information that could offend the sensibility of individuals who were directly or indirectly involved in the events (Maiorana 2013:51). The presence of such an ethical stance is confirmed by the accuracy with which the author handles the testimonies she collected. In the first chapter, for example, Maiorana sketches a portrait of Stefania Noce based on descriptions provided by her parents and by a friend. In order to adhere to the victim's ideals and voice, she also includes the transcription of the article entitled "Ha ancora senso essere femministe?" [Does it still make sense to be a feminist?] that Noce wrote for the local magazine *La bussola*. Furthermore, the writer reconstructs the events that lead to the woman's death by following the version offered by Noce's acquaintances: the tale of the turbulent relationship with Loris Gagliano draws on the words of Stefania's friend Serena, while the femicide is retraced through the memories of the victim's mother – who was chatting at the phone with Stefania and her grandmother when the murder was happening – as well as through that of a neighbor who witnessed the killing from her balcony.

The extensive use of witness accounts does not prevent Maiorana from demonstrating an awareness of the problematic dimension of the testimonial practice. The author seems to be mindful about the aforementioned fallacies of memory and whenever the adherence to the events happens to be particularly elusive because of the strong emotional involvement of the interviewee, she intervenes with the aim of clarifying the relativity, and at the same time the urgency, of her narration. Serena's account, for example, is interrupted by a paragraph where Maiorana explains how difficult the process of memorial reconstruction of painful events can be for the victim's acquaintances and how this state of emotional distress, together with the deceptiveness of retrospective thinking, might affect the act of witnessing (19). Aligning with the ethos that characterizes Levi's approach to memory, the writer still considers testimony a crucial practice with an essential political function that, in the case of gender-based violence, coincides with facilitating a process of recognition and consequent awareness in women who live within abusive relationships by evoking previous experiences of violence (19–20).

In order to fill the narrative spaces left blank by the testimonies, Maiorana decides to adopt two different strategies. On the one hand, she represents pivotal events with accounts based on information provided by the police and by judges, which are generally devoid of personal opinions and impressions. This happens, for example, when the author illustrates the most practical details of the murder (e.g. weapon and cause of death) as well as Gagliano's movements before, during, and after the killing (18;25). On the other hand, Maiorana writes novelized passages that she positions at the beginning of the first, second, and fifth chapters. These sections mainly draw on documented facts, but they also incorporate numerous creative elements and discursive strategies borrowed from the literary tradition.

The opening passage is emblematic. Here Maiorana fictionalizes Noce's actual rescue of a young man lying on the ground in a square in Catania. The representation of the event is preceded by a detailed and lyrical presentation of the surrounding scene where the imminent spring is announced by the first sunny day of the year, which inspires a cheerful atmosphere among the people who crowd the streets. The destabilizing element of the man fainting is then added by the author, who presumes an annoyed and selfish reaction on the passers-by behalf, as they decide to call the police before "going back to eat their ice creams." (8) This attitude is challenged by the presence of a young woman who insists on calling an ambulance and decides to provide her own name and surname to support the man's health care by saying: "You can give my details. [...] My name is Stefania Erminia Noce." (7–8) In this way, Maiorana introduces, with a captivating narrative strategy, the central figure of her biography.

The writer delineates the combinatory strategy she used in this section in the paragraph that follows the opening lines:

> And we don't know if that day, in the spring of 2011, there was that much sun in that particular spot close to a bar in the middle of Catania's city center. We don't even know how many people were on the streets. But we know that Stefania helped that man [...] 'Why do you call the police and not the ambulance instead?' A sentence is enough to make people think. A sentence is enough to change people's actions. And with actions, facts change too. For the better. It couldn't be but a sunny day. (8–9)

The amalgamation of factual and fictional elements contributes here to the portrayal of Noce as an exceptional individual whose altruism differentiates her from the rest of the crowd. The idealization of the victim is rhetorically supported by the epic tones that the writer employs while introducing Noce's identity as well as by the repetitions that, in the last few lines of the excerpt, underline the woman's ability to produce social change. Moreover, the creative process of fictionalization sustains the celebration of the victim through the reference to a symbolic apparatus with strong moral connotations. In particular, the fictitious image of the sun evokes positivity and hope, which are associated with the warm zeal of Noce's personality. The woman, whose commitment as a left-wing and feminist activist is widely mentioned in the text, embodies here the *sol dell'avvenire* [rising sun], emblem of the socialist hope in a future society based on the principle of solidarity.[2] This association is furtherly reinforced by the implicit comparison that Maiorana creates between this scene and the following semi-fictional excerpt, which is centered on the event of Noce's killing and is dominated by the symbolism of the rain. By using this striking opposition, the author guides the emotional participation of the reader toward the recognition of a dualistic moral order.

Once again, the fictionalized representation relies on a significant degree of stereotyping: it backs the construction of the victim as an ideal subject which, in turn, accentuates the brutality of the perpetrator's violence, thus bolstering dichotomization. Interestingly enough, Maiorana's text demonstrates how this rhetorical practice is not only a feature of patriarchal discourse but can be employed in the realm of feminist discourse as well. This is less surprising if we take into account Lippmann's idea of stereotypes as a discursive element that emphasizes sense of community and belonging. Stereotypes can be seen as "an ordered, more or less consistent picture of the world, to which our habits, our tastes, our capacities, our comforts, and our hopes have adjusted themselves. In that world – Lippmann continues – people and things have their well-known places, and do certain expected things. We feel at home there. We fit in. We are members." (1991:90) If, to put that another way, stereotyping is what "fixes in a stable and suggestive image whatever is thought and said," (Amossy and Heidingsfeld 1984:694) a certain degree of stereotypical representation is crucial to the process of mythopoesis, an affirmative component of political activism that aims at creating narratives with the objective of producing imaginaries that support social change. The theorization on mythopoesis – myth formulation, from its Greek etymology – in the areas of art-activism and media-activism in Italy can be led back to the statements of Wu Ming 1, a member of the Bolognese collective of writers Wu Ming, who considered archetype manipulation as an inherently fruitful process for developing a sense of belonging and committed participation to social movements.[3] Maiorana conforms to this practice by portraying Noce as a figure who aligns with the archetype of the positive feminist whose personal and political path toward emancipation was interrupted by sexist violence. This representation is used to sustain the feminist battle against femicide and feeds the readers' sense of injustice.

Following the same inclination to provide an expressive narration that could intrigue the receivers, the author adopts other literary techniques in the continuation of the book. These include strategies previously identified in the newspaper coverage such as suspense narrative and a style borrowed from the horror genre. Suspense is featured at the beginning of the second chapter, when Maiorana depicts the Sicilian town of Licodia Eubea where the murder took place under an unusual rain and "only a few hours before the irreparable." (2013:17) Pickering-Iazzi noticed how suspense in this passage is enhanced by the reiteration of the remark "they do not know," referring to the perspective of Noce's relatives and friends who are not aware of the crime that is about to take place (2018:85). Suspense here functions as a tool that engages the readers at an emotional level on the basis of a moral stance that brings them closer to the victim's perspective. Tension also inspires indignation toward the perpetrator's actions, which are introduced when the suspense structure reaches its closure, as demonstrated by the following quote in which no doubt is left about the man's brutality and guilt: "Today, at 10 o'clock, Stefania will be killed with ten stabbings. The murder weapon will be an 11-centimeter long blade. Loris Gagliano, the self-confessed murderer, will grip it." (Maiorana 2013:18) In light of the aforementioned propensity to blame the victim and excuse the perpetrator criticized by feminists as a feature of the journalistic coverage of femicide, suspense here supplements the counter-informative process and promotes a fair description of the hierarchy imposed by violence. While doing that, however, it also fosters a polarizing rhetoric that fails to highlight the pervasive and integrated dimension of patriarchal culture by portraying the victim and the perpetrator as opposite entities.

Literary references to the horror genre are frequent in the section where Maiorana novelizes the statements of one of the neighbors as well as those of Stefania's mother, Rosa Maiano. Relying on the words of the neighbor, according to whom the victim's blood was dripping from the balcony of Noce's house, the author writes:

> After the call from her mother Gaetana, Rosa rapidly went back home with the police. And she found hell there. Blood everywhere. In the ground floor apartment and in the entrance hall, all over the corridor, in the kitchen, in the living room, on the doors, and the furniture. Even the steps are covered in blood and the walls of the stairs leading to the first floor. Rosa and the police run up and enter the kitchen. Stefania's corpse is lying face-down on the floor by the door that opens on to the small balcony. The blood flows toward the balcony, it melts with the rain and it pours down on the asphalt in via Cairoli. (Maiorana 2013: 24)

The writer insists here on the detail of the blood, which is observed through the perspective of the victim's mother, thus stimulating one of the feelings that, according to Carroll, belongs to the horror genre, revulsion (1990:30), and provoking suspense. This is interesting because the tension and pathos on which horror narratives are based tend to discourage the process of mirroring between reader and characters. Suspense and pathos usually imply the external perspective of the receiver, which is opposed to the internal view of the protagonist. In fact, those who read/watch horror stories usually know more than the characters (think, for example, of the frequently used technique of portraying someone who does not know that they are being followed by a monster/killer) and their emotional responses are shaped on the basis of a process of assimilation to the protagonist's actual or hypothetical reactions, as opposed to empathy (Carroll 1990:95). In other words, when suspense and pathos are involved, receivers are more likely to occupy the position of detached spectators. In Maiorana's case, however, the poetic image of the blood mixing with the rain on the balcony and overflowing from the private dimension of the house into the public sphere of the street demonstrates the attempt to resist the process of spectacularization with a symbolic operation that invites us to consider the femicide experience as a shared public anguish. In this way, the author replaces the separation between the event and the reader with a call for engagement that highlights the social dimension of lethal gender violence.

Quello che resta is characterized by a clear victim-centered perspective that further demonstrates the writer's intention to propose a counter-informative piece aimed at opposing the tendency of periodical journalism to eclipse the woman's experience of violence. The adoption of this specific lens aligns Maiorana's text with feminist discourse and, together with the process of fictionalization, contributes to the construction of an idealized representation of Noce. The aforementioned frequent references to testimonies shared by the victim's relatives or friends foster this type of portrayal because, as opposed to judicial or police statements, these tend to present the murdered subject as an exemplary woman (Gillespie et al. 2013:179). However, in the second part of the book, the author successfully problematizes her own depiction of the protagonist and she manages to do this without renouncing an engaging style that allows the reader a sympathetic participation. At the core of this accomplishment lies the employment of an (inter)subjective narration that activates the receivers' sense of community despite remaining ethically respectful toward the complexity of reality and avoiding simplifications.

One of the last chapters of the text centers on a torchlight procession organized in the streets of Licodia Eubea on December 28, 2012, at the end of the same year that saw feminist movements bringing the issue of femicide to public attention in the wake of cases similar to Noce's killing. The passage showcases a literary style that matches the opening paragraph and the murder section, but on this occasion, Maiorana draws on her own personal experience as a participant in the candlelight vigil instead of making reference to external testimonies. This choice, which highlights her role of witness in the process of community-making that Noce's femicide activated, allows the author to present herself as part of a collectivity of women, thus opening up to the possibility of dialog with the readers. As the following excerpt testifies, the recurring adoption of the personal pronoun "we" – which is declined according to the female gender in the original Italian – serves as a textual reference for this operation and facilitates the receivers' process of mirroring:

> Today we are all Stefania. We were murdered with her. With her we were born anew. Always together, beyond life and death, we pick up what remains, so that nothing will be lost. In this slow and subdued march, the smell of wax that now catches the throat, the soot that makes the eyes itchy, and even the freezing air are like an antidote. It's called "sublimation" and indicates the horror that becomes a teaching, the pain that becomes strength. (Maiorana 2013:46)

Noce's figure is referenced here as the memorial symbol of a struggle against gender violence that concerns all women. It is in the sympathetic dimension of the collective identification with the murdered woman that the possibility of a feminist consciousness (represented by the women who joined the procession) arises. This is clearly indicated not only by the allusion to the isotopy of death and rebirth but also by the analogy of the antidote, which consists of a poetic resymbolization of the violent event as a source of women's political awareness and activism. Moreover, the reproduction of the title expression "quello che resta" (here translated as "what remains") suggests a circular conclusion that, again, presents Noce's legacy as a responsibility for a constant memorial effort that could foster actual engagement against the phenomenon. What clearly emerges here is the ability of the (inter) subjective narration to represent the victim in a multifaceted and problematized way. In fact, Noce is portrayed as an exemplar and an ordinary victim at the same time, as demonstrated by the fact that the recognition of her figure as a symbol for feminist activism does not depend on her excellence, instead, it is deeply rooted in the ordinariness of her life experience as a woman.

Using the same (inter)subjective style, Maiorana also gives an account of the local authorities' decision to remember Noce by naming one of the squares of Licodia Eubea after her. The commemorative act, which took place during the candlelight vigil, included the installation of a plaque with the following inscription: "Stefania Noce (femicide victim) Square." Only a few lines afterwards, the presence of another plaque in one of the rooms of the college attended by Noce, the *Università degli Studi di Catania*, is mentioned. In this case, the caption says: "Stefania Noce, Feminist" (47). The juxtaposition of the two apparently antithetical attributes ("femicide victim" and "feminist") supports the possibility of acknowledging the murdered woman both as an oppressed and active subject, thus overcoming the binary perspective that opposes agency to victimhood.

The representation of the victim proposed in the second part of the text testifies to the possibility of overcoming the problematic aspects of fictionalization (a tendency to make use of dichotomies and, in the case of Maiorana, the glorification of the victim) by using a rhetorical strategy and an (inter)subjective narrative that allows the readers' engagement, thus serving the needs of activism, without supporting the creation of a fixed and rigid image both of the events and of the subjects involved. As Wu Ming 1 recommended, the mythopoetic process activated by the author of *Quello che resta* does not aim at creating crystallized and rigid images (a stereotype), on the contrary, it provides a dynamic and plastic portrayal of Noce as a figure whose complexity can be considered a resource to be adapted to the here and now of activism's narrative needs (Amici 2006:216).

Notwithstanding the numerous positive features, Maiorana's work showcases a rigidly victim-centered approach that does not leave enough space for the description of the perpetrator. As it often happens in the coverage of femicide cases in periodicals, the killer is presented as a "gloomy," "silent, moody, and slightly introverted" subject whose character clashed with that of the "brilliant, sociable, and enthusiastic" Noce (Maiorana 2013:20). The contrastive rhetoric here is the product of a binary logic and it is precisely on the basis of the perpetrator's immorality that his experience is excluded from the discourse. If it is true that Maiorana's choice follows the laudable principle according to which the discursive normativity of patriarchal talk needs to be opposed by an explicitly feminist speech that brings the victim's experience to the fore, it is also obvious that the refusal to tell the perpetrator's story from a feminist perspective deprives the text of a fruitful reflection on the crucial construction of violent masculinity, thus preventing it from the possibility of having an impact on violent men's awareness of gendered abuse.

Notes

1 Now renamed *Generazione, Un altro genere di comunicazione* is a blog managed by media activists who denounce the use of clichéd representations of women, gender nonconforming subjectivities, and childhood in the areas of journalism, advertisement, and the web. On the topic, see the collective's website, https://comunicazionedigenere.wordpress.com/.

2 The success of the image of the *sol dell'avvenire* in Italian left-wing culture dates back to a statement pronounced by one of the leaders of the struggle for the Italian unification, Giuseppe Garibaldi, when he joined the International Working Men's Association (First International) in 1864. After the meetings, Garibaldi described the International as a "rising sun," introducing a metaphor that has proven to be highly productive in the course of Italian political history. Examples of cultural products that reference the expression include the Italian popular song *Fischia il vento*, composed during the Resistance by Felice Cascione on the notes of the Russian song *Katyusha* (Cooke 1997:9) or the recent historical novels by Valerio Evangelisti *Il sole dell'avvenire* (2013).

3 According to Marco Amici, the protean collective of anonymous artists Luther Blisset Project, who were active in the second half of the Nineties in Italy and beyond, were among the groups who consciously adopted the mythopoetic practice as a means of struggle for social change and criticism (2006:215–216). Wu Ming 1 participated in the Luther Blissett Project and further developed the idea of mythmaking in a few pieces, such as the talk on the allegorical significance of the anti-G8 protesters who marched the streets of Genoa in 2001 wearing white tracksuits (*tute bianche*) given in occasion of the Semi(o)resistance festival in Munich (2001) or in the literary essay *New Italian Epic* (2009:97–99).

Works cited

Amici, M. (2006) "La narrazione come mitopoiesi secondo Wu Ming," *Bollettino di Italianistica. Rivista di critica, storia letteraria, filologia e linguistica* 1:184–219.

Amossy, R. and Heidingsfeld, T. (1984) "Stereotypes and Representation in Fiction," *Poetics Today* 4.5:689–700.

Carroll, N. (1990) *The Philosophy of Horror or Paradoxes of the Heart*. New York and London: Routledge.

Cooke, P. (1997) *The Italian Resistance: An Anthology*. Manchester: Manchester University Press.

Gillespie, K. L., Richards, T. N., Givens, E. M., and Smith, D. (2013) "Framing Deadly Domestic Violence: Why the Media Spin Matters in Newspaper Coverage of Femicide," *Violence Against Women* 19(2):222–245.

Giomi, E. (2010) "Neppure con un fiore? La violenza sulle donne nei media italiani," *Il Mulino* 59(6):1001–1009.

Gius, C. and Lalli, P. (2014) "'I Loved Her So Much, but I Killed Her.' Romantic Love as a Representational Frame for Intimate Partner Femicide in Three Italian Newspapers," *Journal for Communication Studies* 7(2):53–75.

Evangelisti, V. (2013) *Il sole dell'avvenire*. Milan: Mondadori.

Lippmann, W. (1991) [1922] *Public Opinion*. New Brunswick and London: Transaction Publishers.

Maiorana, S. (2013) *Quello che resta: storia di Stefania Noce, il femminicidio e i diritti delle donne nell'Italia di oggi*. Villaggio Maori Edizioni: Valverde.

Pickering-Iazzi, R. (2018) "Il femminicidio e il genere nella biografia testimoniale come pratica sociale e simbolica," in Bettaglio, M., Mandolini, N. and Ross, S. (eds.), *Rappresentare la violenza di genere: sguardi femministi tra critica, attivismo e scrittura*. Milan: Mimesis, pp. 71–92.

Wu, M. (2009) *New Italian Epic. Letteratura, sguardo obliquo, ritorno al futuro*. Turin: Einaudi.

Part II

Literary rewritings of *Femminicidio* narratives

5 Between fiction and nonfiction: femicide in Italian literature

The unverifiable and the possible: what do we mean by "Literary"?

The aforementioned tendency toward hybridity that leads to extensive use of faction in journalism is coupled with a growing predisposition of literary texts to include explicit or implicit references to the methods of journalistic research. As we have already seen mentioning the *reportage narrativo*, there are many examples of writers who worked both as journalists and literati in the context of twentieth-century Italy. However, it is only from the 1990s onwards, according to critics of Italian literature (Donnarumma 2008:49–52; Palumbo Mosca 2011:216–218; Ricciardi 2011), that literary narratives published in the peninsula have showcased a growing and clear interest in the methods of documentary and testimonial writing, which has resulted in the presence of increasing (though often not unambiguous) references to the practice. The recognition of this inclination, which was labeled *ritorno alla realtà* [return to reality] following the publication of a special issue of the academic journal *Allegoria* entirely dedicated to the topic (Donnarumma et al. 2008), allowed scholars to (re)question the rigid disciplinary boundaries between journalism and literature.

Notwithstanding this undeniable and (most of the time) fruitful adulteration, the practice of addressing reality through literature maintains a specificity which, as Raffaello Palumbo Mosca pointed out, is linked to the "peculiar novelistic tension toward the realization of a human truth" that "surpasses every ambition to adhere to facts." (2017:35) Similarly, Raffaele Donnarumma stated that "what identifies literature is not its claim for truth but, more modestly, its collocation beyond the realm of verifiability." (2011a:30) In other words, the literary approach differs from the journalistic one because it focuses on the representation of dynamics, phenomena, and events that cannot be

DOI: 10.4324/9781003120339-5

substantiated. On a similar note, Alberto Casadei argued that literature operates on the domain of the possible even when it incorporates journalistic practices. In this sense, it opens up spaces governed by an ethos that transcends the direct relationship with facts, thus allowing an imagining of new and alternative eventualities (Casadei 2007:119–120).

In the wake of these reflections and of their implications for the representation of a sensitive phenomenon such as femicide, this volume distinguishes between journalistic (first part) and literary narratives (second part). This separation and the consequent decision to assign the considered works to one part or the other was guided by the presence in the texts of narrative strategies that explore the literary dimensions of the unverifiable and the possible, or lack thereof. As the analysis conducted in the previous chapters demonstrates, inquiries such as *Se questi sono gli uomini* and *Quello che resta* juxtapose the exposition of documentable events and creative narrative sketches that challenge the principle of objective journalism, thus approaching the sphere of the unverifiable. However, these elements do not undermine the dominant informative approach that characterizes the two books. The same can be said for the literary dimension of the possible, which is slightly touched upon in the final parts of Iacona and Maiorana's texts, where the prospect of change is envisaged but does not substitute the works' overall descriptive approach with an imaginative one aimed at reshaping the perimeter of the femicide story. Therefore, references to the realm of the possible and unverifiable must be constant and constitutive of the text for the works to be included in this part.

The first work analyzed here, *Fiore… come me. Storie di dieci vite spezzate* [Flower… Like Me. Stories of Ten Broken Lives] (2013), for example, is a hybrid short-stories collection in which the author, Giuliana Covella, adopts a narratological perspective that coincides with that of the murdered woman, thus overcoming the barriers of realist writing as well as the strict testimonial method of journalistic narrative. Conversely, the anthology *Nessuna più* [No One More] (2013), edited by Marilù Oliva, reworks true stories of femicide with a declared nondocumentary approach, while in *La scuola cattolica* [The Catholic School] (2016) Edoardo Albinati references a historical event that he indirectly experienced during his teenage years (the aforementioned Circeo Slaughter) through an autofictional lens that explicitly confronts with unverifiability and creativity as notions that expand the realm of the possible. The last text considered, *Padreterno* [Heavenly Father] (2016) by Caterina Serra, adopts a completely fictional outlook and rewrites a mythological story of lethal gendered violence (that of Aristaeus) without the limits imposed by the need to adhere to facts.

Feminist rewritings

This corpus of literary texts is the result of a selection among the publications on the topic of femicide that have reached Italian bookshops since 2012. After a careful consultation of the numerous volumes (novels or short-story collections) published after the mainstreaming of feminist discourse on lethal gender violence, two major tendencies have been identified. On the one hand, many Italian works on femicide can be labeled as rewritings of previous journalistic, historical, or mythical narratives. On the other hand, books belonging to the area of genre fiction (crime, horror, and science fiction) are a largely represented category when it comes to Italian texts on women's sexist murders.[1] Considering the ability of rewritings of (true and not true) stories of femicide to support a critical reflection on the issue of fictional and non-fictional portrayals of gender abuse that this volume aims at conducting, this category was selected for the analysis. Moreover, literary rewritings present a higher degree of proximity with journalistic narratives, which facilitates the comparative methodology that characterizes this book.

The idea of rewriting that serves as a unifying conceptual tool for the texts examined in this second part testifies to the propensity of the literary works to renegotiate and deconstruct narratives that were already rooted in individual and collective memory. This tendency can be referred to the need for implementing the criticism of mainstream and canonical narratives developed by the feminist metadiscourse on femicide and, as such, it can be compared to the counter-informative ethos that guides the journalistic inquiries discussed in the previous chapters. But literary rewriting is, as Liedeke Plate argued, first of all, a feminist practice through which women[2] have been able to (re)appropriate stories and events with the objective of performing their memorial and at the same time transformative urgency (2010:7–8). In this sense, rewriting re-situates women within the mechanisms of cultural memory production and, consequently, it presents them as subjects whose agency is expressed by their capacity for contrasting patriarchal monologism (Plate 2010:5–6). As Adrienne Rich contended, "feminist re-vision" is nothing less than a survival strategy for the feminist subjectivity (1972:18).

In the Italian context, rewriting has been an essential practice for feminists who have been active within and beyond the literary sphere. The redrafting of journalistic chronicles on violence against women, for example, was a constitutive part of the cultural work that feminist activists undertook during the Seventies, when the aforementioned

Circeo massacre occurred and sexual violence became a publicly debated political issue (Mandolini 2017:428–429). The critical renarration of the journalistic coverage of rape cases produced in those years is testified, among other examples, by Maria Adele Teodori's *Le violentate* (1977), a publication where the author rewrites two episodes of sexual violence from a feminist perspective (the Circeo massacre and a rape that occurred in Verona in 1976) as well as the trials and protests that followed.

It is again during the Seventies that the rewriting of historical events developed among feminists in Italy. The aim of reassigning protagonism to female historical figures obliterated by patriarchal historiography characterizes texts such as *La Resistenza taciuta* [The Silenced Resistence] (1976), with which Anna Maria Bruzzone and Rachele Farina brought to the surface the "silenced" participation of women to the struggle against Fascism in the Piedmont region, or *La signora del gioco* [The Lady of the Game] (1976), a feminist reading by Luisa Muraro of the historical phenomenon of witch-hunting. Later, in the Eighties, the theories on feminist historiography elaborated in the Anglophone cultural context by scholars such as Natalie Zemon-Davies (1976) were introduced in Italy, stimulating the emergence of a national debate on the issues (Addis Saba et al. 1992:118) as well as the production of numerous feminist historical novels (Lazzaro-Weis 1993:121–122).

The same rewriting attitude can be found in Italian women thinkers' tendency to rework mythical narratives with the objective of crafting feminist parables. Here it is imperative to mention the Veronese collective of philosophers Diotima – the name is a tribute to the Greek prophetess Diotima of Mantinea – and one if its members, Adriana Cavarero, who authored the volume *Nonostante Platone* [Notwithstanding Plato] (1990), where stories of women taken from classical mythology and philosophy are reinterpreted with the aim of "'restoring' a female symbolic order that has been cancelled for millennia." (Cavarero 2009:20) Even in this case, the activity of Diotima derives from the mythical rewritings started by feminists at an international level and, in particular, by French thinkers such as Monique Wittig (1969), Luce Irigaray (1974), and Hélène Cixous (2010).

Italian rewritings on gender violence

Beyond being a crucial practice in the area of Italian feminist activism, theory, and scholarly work, the rewriting of journalistic, historical, and mythical narratives is a tendency even in Italian literary prose on the topic of gender-based violence throughout the twentieth century. The revision of personal and collective stories marked by episodes of sexist persecution is at the core of quite a few literary works belonging to the tradition of Italian women's writing, including *Avanti il divorzio* [Pro Divorce] (1902) by Anna Franchi and *Una donna* [A Woman] (1906) by Sibilla Aleramo, two texts that compete among critics for the label of first Italian feminist novel (Gallucci 1999:371; Gragnani 2011:112–113; Nozzoli 1978:36; Polselli 1999:102–103; Wood 1995:75). Both Franchi and Aleramo's works are literary reformulations of the authors' emancipation from the vexations suffered within the family. As such, they can be considered re-narrations of life events aimed at opposing the official side of the story proposed by patriarchal authorities (mainly legal ones) interested in preserving the institution of marriage. *Avanti il divorzio* and *Una donna* entertain a problematic relationship with the idea of truth, thus conforming to the model of women's auto/biography proposed by Liz Stanley, according to which truth is a principle that cannot but be constantly renegotiated by an emerging and mobile subject (women) who, nevertheless, demands to be acknowledged (1995:61). This characteristic, which relates to the discussion on fictional and nonfictional representations of femicide proposed in this section, is exhibited by Franchi, who rejects any positivistic idea of authenticity and repeatedly defines her storytelling practice as an exercise of "humble truth" (2012:11; 241) instead. Aleramo, for her part, omits from her life stories a few details that she will subsequently reveal in her following autobiographical work, *Il passaggio* [The Passage] (1919). In addition, she decides not to unveil the protagonist's name, a choice that grants exemplarity and universality to the story (Jacobs 56), but that transgresses the "autobiographical pact," (Lejeune 1975:23–24) thus casting doubts on the narration's truthfulness.

If the semi-autobiographical novel of awakening (Felski 1989:127–142; Rosowski 1979) is the genre that provided the structure for the rewriting of personal life stories of abuse, the historical novel offered women writers who delved into the issue of sexist violence the opportunity to reshape patriarchal accounts of past events. Already recognized as milestones among the works produced by Italian women writers, *Artemisia* (1947) by Anna Banti, and *La Storia* [History] (1974) by Elsa Morante, are experimental historical novels dealing with the issue of rape.[3] Banti's work, a hybrid text in which the historical novel meets the auto/biographical mode, retraces the story of Artemisia Gentileschi (1593–1656), a baroque painter active between Florence, Naples, and London, and of the sexual violence she suffered in her adolescence. Despite being the result of meticulous archival documentation, the novel is structured as a long monologue through which the author imaginatively addresses Artemisia and openly reveals her dubitative approach according to which the act of narrative is always the result of a creative and subjective supposition, instead of a descriptive operation (Guerricchio 1997:73). This is coupled with Banti's manipulation of some crucial events of the painter's life, such as the composition of one of her last works, *Self Portrait as the Allegory of Painting* (1638–1639), which the writer reimagines as the portrait of one of Artemisia's fellow female artists, Annella De Rosa, who was killed by her husband. As critics have noticed, in *Artemisia*, the opposition to patriarchal historiography can be realized only through fiction, the realm of the possible where Banti relocates the obliterated reality of women's presence in the art scene and their resistance to the continuum of sexist discriminations (Cannon 1994:326; Craig 2010:604; Scarparo 2002:368).

The act of contrasting patriarchal historical narratives by means of a literary operation, connects *Artemisia* to *La Storia*, a bestselling novel set in the months of Rome's occupation by the Nazis and built on the interlocking of small fictional stories aimed at deconstructing the monolithic and universalizing framework of traditional historiography (Gioanola 2005:356; Oram 2003:410; Serkowska 2006:379). The subversive role of the fictional (Della Coletta 1996:117) manifests itself in Morante's ability to sketch complex relational dynamics that transcend (and thus challenge) the stringent opposition between victims and perpetrators proposed in chronicles (Lucamante 2015:100). In this regard, there are three micro-stories where episodes of gendered violence are told: the rape of the Jewish protagonist, Ida, by the German soldier Gunther, which opens the novel; the sexual violence and femicide of Mariulina and her mother during a Nazis reprisal; the femicide of the prostitute Santina by hands of her pimp and lover Nello D'Angeli. In each of the aforementioned episodes, Morante deals with the issue of abuse toward women by describing and, at the same time, reimagining the historical and social relationships of domination between genders and classes. The initial scene of rape, for example, was interpreted by the critic as the story of subjugation and subsequent empowerment of Ida (Oram 2003:421), while Santina's murder was labeled as a tale that challenges the Manichean depiction of perpetrators proposed by journalistic and judicial official reports (Mandolini 2017b).

Despite the productivity of women's rewritings of life and historical chronicles, mythological rewriting is the area that, according to Plate, inaugurated the practice of feminist manipulation of canonical narratives (2010:6–7). In fact, mythology offers a paradigm for the re-writing activity, because its inclination to repetition is the essential requirement for a tale's reproduction as the same and simultaneously different, which is precisely what feminist revision pursues by passing on and, concurrently, contesting cultural memory (Plate 2010:29–31). It is not by coincidence then, that mythological rewriting occupies a crucial role in Italian feminist literature on gender violence, especially since the 1990s, which is to say after the philosophical re-visions carried out by Diotima. *La lunga vita di Marianna Ucrìa* [The Silent Duchess] (1990) by Dacia Maraini and *L'amore molesto* [Troubling Love] (1991) by Elena Ferrante are the most renowned Italian novels covering the topic of statuary rape and repressed memory through implicit references to classical mythology. Maraini's work is a fictionalized reconstruction of the writer's foremother (Marianna Ucrìa) that can be read as the re-vision of the Greek myth of Philomela (Brooke 1995:191–192); Ferrante's novel, on the other hand, is a non-disclosed rewriting of the myth of Demeter and Persephone (De Rogatis 2016). In both cases, the myth is adjusted to the needs of the feminist symbolic operation: Maraini removes from the story of Philomela the vindictive dimension and creates for her protagonist a revenge based on personal liberation (Brooke 1995:196–198); Ferrante uses the myth as a palimpsest to insert a criticism of patriarchal doxic narratives such as that which covered the sexual violence suffered by the protagonist when she was a child.

Fiction vs nonfiction

As the aforementioned examples demonstrate, the practice of literary rewriting includes entirely fictional texts as well as narratives based on explicit references to real events (what is commonly referred to as literary nonfiction). Critics who have studied the fiction versus nonfiction issue have rightly argued that it is no longer desirable to draw a sharp line between the two categories because, as poststructuralist theories taught us, narratives (even the so-called nonfictonal ones) always reformulate events, regardless of the author's intention to adhere to them (Donnarumma 2011a:31–32; Boscolo and Jossa 2014:19; Palumbo Mosca 2011:210). In this sense, all accounts are intrinsically fictional, given their inability to reproduce reality and its complexities thoroughly. However, readers belonging to our hypermodern epoch[4] still rely on the separation between fiction and nonfiction to distinguish narratives that have a clear derivative relationship with reality from creative tales that are ethically unhooked from the imperative of adherence to "truth." As John Searle noticed (1975:221–232), this separation is merely a conventional one and, despite not being able to guarantee the text's truthful operation, it establishes with the reader a new "pact based on an ethical will of understanding and intervention." (Donnarumma 2011a: 49) In other words, it communicates to the receivers of non-fictional texts the author's intention to establish a link with factuality.

It is precisely on this reading pact that many narrative experiments produced in Italy since the 1990s are based. The previously outlined interest of contemporary Italian writers for a restored political and ethical relationship with reality resulted in the publication of numerous hybrid texts[5] where literary practice melts with journalistic, sociological, or anthropological strategies employed to perform memorial or counter-informative needs (Ricciardi 2011:183). But this documental approach does not coincide with the positivist and naturalist idea of *mimesis*. On the contrary, it is based on a dialog with the event that is necessarily mediated by a subjective filter. It goes without saying that, in the visible intricate of fact and fiction that characterizes Italian contemporary novels, truth is a polymorphous rather than a monolithic entity, which lies in each one (of the many) possible counter-stories and in the symbolic generalizations constructed with the help of literature (Palumbo Mosca 2011:210).

This critical engagement with the real can be compared to the approach that, before the emergence of hypermodern tendencies in Italian literary prose, feminist writers employed to counterbalance their deconstructionist verve toward the patriarchal with an ethical relationship to the idea of truth (Felski 1989:70–78). This attitude is particularly evident in the case of literature on gendered violence which, as we have already seen, has frequently revised patriarchal grand narratives by proposing counter-stories guided by a positioned, but nonetheless politically effective, tendency to authenticity. A roaring case in this sense is *Isolina* (1980) by Dacia Maraini, a novel based on the true events of Isolina Canuti's death in Verona in 1900 as a result of a forced botched abortion. Maraini's reconstruction of the facts that led to the femicide and to the obliteration of Isolina from the historical chronicles of Verona is carried out with the aim of re-assigning representative space to the figure of a woman who was silenced by patriarchal violence. For this reason, the narrative proves to be extremely faithful to the sources and the documentary traces that permit to bring Isolina back to the present light (Hanafin 2010:208). At the same time, however, Maraini's tale clearly exhibits the author/

narrator's personal involvement and comments, which act like diegetic elements that help in the process of assembling the story's pieces and allow to inscribe Isolina's tragedy into the socio-political present from which the narrative stems (Cannon 2006:45–58).

If literary nonfiction engages in a problematic but nonetheless solid relationship with the reality of gendered violence and femicide, fictional narratives (or narratives where the degree of unverifiability is higher) do not refrain from the act of critically recalling the model offered by a contemporary social and political discourse on the topic. The actualizations of mythical narratives already cited offer an example in this regard. In this sub-genre, literary fiction is used to represent socially relevant issues such as sexist violence (see Maraini's and Ferrante's texts) with the general aim of contributing to the discursive reelaboration of the phenomenon by means of a manipulation of patriarchal rhetoric and symbolism.

The following pages are dedicated to the analysis of four readaptations of stories that were either obscured by patriarchal chronicles or already (but problematically) included in cultural memory and common imaginary. Despite showcasing a common interest in providing the reader with experiments of re-vision, the works exhibit a different degree of fictionality. It is by taking this specific aspect into consideration that the texts will be analyzed and ordered. Therefore, the main objective of this section is to observe how the representation of a sensitive phenomenon such as femicide differs between narratives based on true events and creative texts that are not aimed at dealing with actual facts.

Notes

1 These include *La notte alle mie spalle* (2012) and *Cosa resta di noi* (2015) by Giampaolo Simi, *La costola di Adamo* (2014) by Antonio Manzini, *Il basilico di Palazzo Galletti* (2018) by Giuseppina Torregrossa, *Le spose sepolte* (2018) by Marilù Oliva, the anthology *Rosa sangue* (2016), edited by Donato Altomare and Loredana Pietrafesa, *Avrai i miei occhi* (2020) by Nicoletta Vallorani.

2 Women are not the only social group that has resorted to rewriting. As Julie Sanders pointed out, the practice of textual "appropriation" is extensively used among marginalized subjectivities to subvert and criticize dominant narratives (2006:8–9).

3 Other historical novels addressing the topic of gender violence include *Lucrezia Borgia* (1931) by Maria Bellonci, *La ciociara* (1957) by Alberto Moravia, *La chimera* (1990) by Sebastiano Vassalli, *La lunga vita di Marianna Ucrìa* (1990) by Dacia Maraini, and *La briganta* (1990) by Maria Rosa Cutrufelli.

4 The category of hypermodernity was introduced by the French sociologist Gilles Lipovetsky and it was later adapted to the field of Italian literary studies by Raffaele Donnarumma, who used the label to describe the cultural phase that followed the postmodernist one. The main characteristics of this time are the persistence of a distrust for grand narratives inaugurated during the postmodern age but a renewed interest for the real, a revived will to produce social impact and to critically retrieve the concepts of "truth" and "subjectivity" (Donnarumma 2011b:18–21).

5 The most prominent text in this regard is *Gomorra* (2006) by Roberto Saviano.

Works cited

Addis, Saba, M., Noack, S. and Levin, T. (1992) "Women's Studies in Italy: The Story of Feminist Historiography," *Women's Studies Quarterly* 20(3–4):116–126.

Aleramo, S. (1985) [1919] *Il passaggio*. Milan: Serra e Riva.

Aleramo, S. (2013) [1906] *Una donna*. Milan: Feltrinelli.

Altomare, D. and Pietrafesa, L. (2016) *Rosa sangue: un'antologia fantastica per raccontare il femminicidio*. Matera: Altrimedia.

Banti, A. (1989) [1947] *Artemisia*. Milan: Rizzoli.

Bellonci, M. (1998) [1931] *Lucrezia Borgia*. Milan: Mondadori.

Boscolo, C. and Jossa, S. (2014) "Finzioni metastoriche e sguardi politici della narrativa contemporarnea," in Boscolo, C. and Jossa, S. (eds.), *Scritture di resistenza. Sguardi politici dalla narrative italiana contemporanea*. Rome: Carocci, pp. 15–65.

Brooke, G. (1995) "Sicilian Philomelas: Marianna Ucrìa and the Muted Women of her Time," *Italian Culture* 13(1):201–211.

Bruzzone, A. M. and Farina, R. (1976) *La resistenza taciuta. Dodici vite di partigiane piemontesi*. Milan: La Pietra.

Cannon, J. (1994) "Artemisia and the Life Story of the Exceptional Woman," *Forum Italicum* 28(2):322–341.

Cannon, J. (2006) *The Novel as Investigation. Leonardo Sciascia, Dacia Maraini and Antonio Tabucchi*. Toronto, Buffalo, London: University of Toronto Press.

Casadei, A. (2007) *Stile e tradizione nel romanzo italiano contemporaneo*. Bologna: Il Mulino.

Cavarero, A. (2009) [1990] *Nonostante Platone. Figure femminili nella filosofia antica*. Verona: Ombre Corte.

Cixous, H. (2010) [1975] *Le rire de la Méduse*. Paris: Galilée.

Craig, S. (2010) "Translation and Treachery: Historiography and the Betrayal of Meaning in Anna Banti's *Artemisia*," *Italica* 87(4):602–618.

Cutrufelli, M. R. (2005) [1990]. *La briganta*. Milan: Sperling e Kupfer.

Della Coletta, C. (1996) *Plotting the Past. Metamorphoses of Historical Narrative in Modern Italian Fiction*. West Lafayette: Purdue University Press.

De Rogatis, T. (2016) "Metamorphosis and Rebirth: Greek Mythology and Initiation Rites in Elena Ferrante's *Troubling Love*," in Russo Bullaro, G. and Love, S. (eds.), *The Works of Elena Ferrante. Reconfiguring the Margins.* New York: Palgrave, pp. 185–206.

Donnarumma, R. (2008) "Nuovi realismi e persistenze postmoderne: narratori italiani di oggi," *Allegoria* 57:26–54.

Donnarumma, R. (2011a) "Angosce di derealizzazione. Non-fiction e fiction nella narrativa italiana di oggi," in Serkovska, H. (ed.), *Finzione, cronaca, realtà. Scambi, intrecci e prospettive nella narrativa italiana contemporanea.* Massa: Transeuropa, pp. 23–50.

Donnarumma, R. (2011b) "Ipermodernità: ipotesi per un congedo dal postmoderno," *Allegoria* 64:15–50.

Donnarumma, R., Policastro, G. and Taviani, G. (eds.) (2008) "Ritorno alla realtà? Narrativa e cinema alla fine del postmoderno," *Allegoria* 57.

Felski, R. (1989) *Beyond Feminist Aesthetics. Feminist Literature and Social Change*. London: Hutchinson Radius.

Ferrante, E. (1991) *L'amore molesto*. Rome: e/o.

Franchi, A. (2012) [1902] *Avanti il divorzio*. Florence: Sandron.

Gallucci, C. C. (1999) "The Body and the Latter: Sibilla Aleramo in the Interwar Years," *Forum Italicum* 33(2):363–391.

Gioanola, E. (2005) *Psicanalisi e interpretazione letteraria*. Milan: Itaca.

Gragnani, C. (2011) "Un io titanico per un'"umile verità': ideologia e disegno letterario in Avanti il divorzio di Anna Franchi," in Frau, O. and Garagnani, C. (eds.), *Sottoboschi letterari: sei case studies fra Otto e Novecento*. Florence: Firenze University Press, pp. 85–113.

Guerricchio, R. (1997). 'Vite vere e immaginarie di Anna Banti Laopera di Anna Banti. in Biagini, E. (ed), *L'opera di Anna Banti. Atti del convegno di studi a Firenze, 8–9 maggio 1992*, Verona: Olshki, pp. 75–89.

Hanafin, P. (2010) "An Ethics for Dead Voices: Law and the Politics of Sexual Difference in Dacia Maraini's *Isolina*." *Law and Humanities* 4(2):195–209.

Irigaray, L. (1974). '*Speculum'. De laautre femme*. Paris: Minuit.

Jacobs, S. (1993) "In Search of the Other's Subjectivity in the Works of Sibilla Aleramo," in Arkinstall, C. (ed.), *Literature and Quest*. Amsterdam and Atlanta: Rodopi, pp. 53–64.

Lazzaro-Weis, C. (1993) *From Margins to Mainstream. Feminism and Fictional Modes in Italian Women's Writing, 1968–1990*. Philadelphia: University of Pennsylvania Press.

Lejeune, P. (1975) *Le pact autobiographique*. Paris: Seuil.

Lucamante, S. (2015) "'The World Must Be the Writer's Concern': Elsa Morante's Vision of History," in Lucamante, S. (ed.), *Elsa Morante's Politics of Writing. Rethinking Subjectivity, History, and the Power of Art*. Madison and Teaneck: Fairleigh Dickinson University Press, pp. 87–103.

Mandolini. N. (2017a) "Beyond Rape: Dacia Maraini's *Donna in guerra* and Maria Schiavo's *Macellum* in the 1970s Italian Debate on Gender Violence," *Italian Studies* 72(4):428–442.

Mandolini. N. (2017b) "Il femminicidio raccontato in *Artemisia* di Anna Banti e *La Storia* di Elsa Morante." in Alfonzetti, B., Cancro, T., Di Iasio, V. and Pietrobon, E. (eds.), *L'italianistica oggi: ricerca e didattica. Atti del XIX Congresso dell'ADI*. Roma: ADI editore: https://www.italianisti.it/pubblicazioni/atti-di-congresso/laitalianistica-oggi-ricerca-e-didattica/Art_%20Mandolini-Atti%20ADI%202015.pdf Accessed 22 January 2021.

Maraini, D. (1980) *Isolina: la donna tagliata a pezzi*. Milan: Rizzoli.

Maraini, D. (1990) *La lunga vita di Marianna Ucrìa*. Milan: Rizzoli.

Maraini, D. (1999) [1990] *La lunga vita di Marianna Ucría*. Milan: Rizzoli.

Manzini, A. (2014) *La costola di Adamo*. Palermo: Sellerio.

Morante, E. (1995) [1974] *La storia*. Turin: Einaudi.

Moravia, A. (2001) [1957] *La ciociara*. Milan: Bompiani.

Muraro, L. (1976) *La signora del gioco. La caccia alle streghe interpretata dalle sue vittime*. Milan: La Tartaruga.

Nozzoli, A. (1978) *Tabù e coscienza. La letteratura femminile in Italia tra Ottocento e Novecento*. Florence: La Nuova Italia.

Oliva, M. (2018) *Le spose sepolte*. Milan: Harper Collins.

Oram, L. (2003) "Rape, Rupture and Revision: Visionary Imagery and Historical Reconstrucion in Elsa Morante's *La Storia*," *Forum Italicum* 37(2):409–435.

Palumbo Mosca, R. (2011) "Narrazioni spurie: letteratura della realtà nell'Italia contemporanea," *MLN* 126(1):200–223.

Palumbo Mosca, R. (2017) "Oltre l'idea di realismo. Scrittori della vita nel nuovo millennio. Primi appunti," *Heteroglossia* 14:29–38.

Plate, L. (2010) *Transforming Memories in Women's Contemporary Rewriting*. New York: Palgrave.

Polselli, P. (1999) "*Una donna* di Sibilla Aleramo. Ovvero come conciliare arte, vita, fantesche e donne metafisiche," *The Italianist* 19(1):101–129.

Ricciardi, S. (2011) "'Gomorra' e l'estetica documentale nel nuovo millennio," *Interférences Littéraires* 7:167–186.

Rich, A. (1972) "When We Dead Awaken: Writing as Re-Vision," *College English* 34(1):18–30.

Rosowski, S. (1979) "The Novel of Awakening in Studies in the Novel," *Genre Norman NY* 12(3):313–332.

Sanders, J. (2006) *Adaptation and Appropriation*. New York: Routledge.

Saviano, R. (2006) *Gomorra*. Milan: Mondadori.

Scarparo, S. (2002) "Artemisia: The Invention of a 'Real' Woman," *Italica* 79(3):363–378.

Searle, J. R. (1975) "The Logical Status of Fictional Discourse," *New Literary History* 6(2):319–332.

Serkowska, H. (2006) "About One of the Most Disputed Literary Cases of the Seventies: Elsa Morante's *La Storia*," *Italianistica Utraiectina* 1:372–386.

Simi, G. (2012) *La notte alle mie spalle*. Rome: e/o.

Simi, G. (2015) *Cosa resta di noi*. Palermo: Sellerio.

Stanley, L. (1995) *The Auto/biographical I: The Theory and Practice of Feminist Auto/Biography*. Manchester: Manchester University Press.
Teodori, M. A. (1977) *Le violentate*. Milan: SugarCo.
Torregrossa. G. (2018) *Il basilico di palazzo Galletti*. Milan: Mondadori.
Vassalli, S. (2015) [1990] *La chimera*. Milan: Rizzoli.
Vallorani, N. (2020) *Avrai i miei occhi*. Modena: Zona42.
Wittig, M. (1969) *Les Guérillères*. Paris: Minuit.
Wood, S. (1995) *Italian Women's Writing 1869–1994*. London: A&C Black.
Zemon-Davies, N. (1976) "Women's History. Transition: The European's Case," *Feminist Studies* 3(3-4):83–103.

6 Rewriting journalistic narratives: *Fiore… come me* (2013) by Giuliana Covella and *Nessuna più* (2013), edited by Marilù Oliva

This chapter gathers the analysis of two short-story collections published in 2013, both aimed at renarrating journalistic accounts of femicide stories: *Fiore… come me* by Giuliana Covella and *Nessuna più*, edited by Marilù Oliva. Despite the fact that both texts revise the narration of events that had been brought to the attention of the public through the news, the works showcase a different degree of fictionality that facilitates a comparison and a subsequent reflection on how this variation affects the representation of episodes of lethal gender violence as well as readers' potential identification with them.

Published by the Neapolitan Spazio Creativo, *Fiore… come me. Storie di dieci vite spezzate* by the emerging journalist Giuliana Covella is a book directed at a potentially vast readership whose stated aim is to raise awareness on the phenomenon of femicide. Despite its limited and local distribution, the work became object of critical discussions on the topic of femicide and testimonial biography (Pickering-Iazzi 2018). It includes short pieces dedicated to the stories of ten women murdered in Naples and two extra contents: an interview with the lawyer Elena Coccia and a brief commentary by the journalist Francesca Scognamiglio. *Fiore… come me* explicitly engages with the practice of rewriting journalistic narratives, as is made clear in the volume's introduction written by the journalist Paolo Siani, who discloses the aim of the text to qualify as an alternative to the ephemeral femicide accounts provided by periodical journalism (2013:12–13).

Notwithstanding this statement, Covella's work is a text whose collocation proves difficult, given its high degree of hybridization between investigative journalism and literature. On the one side, the author is presented as a journalist in the introduction as well as in the cover bio. Moreover, a documentary approach is clearly revealed by the presence of a brief informative piece located at the end of each story, where a picture of the dead woman and details on the femicidal

DOI: 10.4324/9781003120339-6

event are provided. On the other hand, the narrative in *Fiore… come me* consistently relies on the adoption of a notably literary device: the choice of assigning the role of narrator to the dead woman. According to Alice Bennett, the adoption of the so-called technique of the dead narrator, which challenges the practical impossibility of giving an account of one's own death using a first-person narrative, necessarily implies an allusion to the realm of fiction (2012:103). In fact, the ventriloquist effect produced by the employment of this strategy deviates the reader's focus from the sphere of the real, which is typically addressed by journalists, to the field of the (im)possible that characterizes the literary. The act of overcoming the limitations imposed by the real does not imply a complete departure from the realist mode, which in Covella's text is testified by a general respect for the principle of verisimilitude. In this sense, *Fiore… come me* belongs to the literary category of hybrid realism (Ercolino 2015:249–263), a narrative mode characterized by the interest in remaining credibly attached to the phenomenon while concurrently blurring the constraints of the realistic and the possible.

The presence of a strong literary component, the same that determined the inclusion of the texts in this part of the volume, is not addressed by the author, who makes no reference to the partiality of her narrative practice nor to the ethical obstacles of appropriating the victim's voice. Given the text's high level of hybridity and the author's stated career in the field of journalism, this omission proves problematic because it prevents the implicit pact with the reader to be fair. It is precisely in light of this lack that the testimonial biographies in *Fiore… come me* offer a potentially misleading image to the readers and, as Robin Pickering-Iazzi noted, run the risk of re-silencing the dead women to whom they aim at re-donating a voice (2018:91–92). As we will see in the next paragraphs, Covella's authorial transparency is particularly critical because of the author's recurring habit of combining the technique of the dead narrator with the exhibition of presumed but unverifiable thoughts of the victim that most of the time also contribute to presenting the women as idealized but stereotypical figures.

It is not surprising, then, that *Fiore… come me* displays critical elements even on a thematic level. Not all the cases selected for the rewriting, for example, can be classified as femicides. The volume includes the stories of Matilde Sorrentino and Teresa Buonocore, both killed after denouncing pedophilic acts carried out on their children, as well as those of Mena Morlando and Palma Scamardella, who were inadvertently murdered during organized crime ambushes. This demonstrates that gender-related killings are not the criteria employed for selecting the murder cases. On the contrary, the sex of the murdered women and their status of innocent victims guides the choice, which testifies to the essentialist approach characterizing the collection.

The analysis of Covella's work also exhibits a tendency to offer a portrayal of the victims that conforms to patriarchal gender roles. This is the result of a process of idealization that, as scholars who studied the representation of abused women pointed out, often relies on rhetorical practices of stereotyping and exclusion, such as the implicit discursive separation between the good/innocent women and the bad/guilty ones (Christie 1986; Benedict 1992; Greer 2007:22–25). For example, the femicide victim Emiliana Femiano is described as a young woman whose frivolous appearance disguised a caring personality, as confirmed by her charitable gesture of bringing food to Neapolitan homeless at Christmas (Covella 2013:16–17). The visually impaired and extremely poor Enza Cappuccio, on the other hand, is constructed as an ideal victim by means of infantilizing discursive techniques that depict her as innocent. In line with the patriarchal representation of the feminine and the disabled as weak subjects who need protection (Fine and Asch 1981; Thomson 1997), Covella imposes her idealizing gaze on the figure of Enza and employs the problematic ventriloquist effect to have the woman say: "I have always thought that those who cannot see have the soul of a child inside." (Covella 2013:26) Another problematic example is offered by the story of Florinda Di Marino, a primary school teacher killed by her partner. In Covella's semi-fictional realm, Florinda talks about herself and says: "My soul is pure, yes. It is not me saying it. It's what other people say." (36) The ventriloquist technique is used here to amplify the idealizing outcome that generally results from the employment of references to testimonies provided by the victim's friends and family members (Binik 2015:400–401).

The idealizing and stereotypically gendered representation of the victims is clearly displayed by the frequent connection of the women's image to that of the good mother, which is often represented as an essential trait of female subjectivity. In the piece about Emiliana, for example, the association between femininity, motherhood, and violence is conveyed by the juxtaposition of the story of Regina, a dog who recovered from a difficult labor thanks to her untamed vitality, with that of the femicide victim, who survived a first attack by her ex-partner aided by her *joie de vivre* (Covella 2013:21). This textual concordance appears even more relevant in light of Covella's description of Emiliana as a young woman whose biggest desire is a future as a mother (19). In the narrative, the vitality that characterizes the figure of Regina as well as that of Emiliana is irremediably linked to the idea of motherhood; moreover, the comparison between the sexist violence suffered by the woman and the natural suffering of labor contributes to the problematic portrayal of pain as a constitutive component of women's lives.

In Matilde Sorrentino's story, maternity emerges again as an ineludible feature for female subjects, thus fostering an essentialist interpretation of gender issues. Matilde, writes Covella, only "knew a single truth: that of being a mother" (46) and her role as mother defines her life as much as her death, which happened as a result of the official complaints made about the pedophilic attacks experienced by her children. The ambush that led to Matilde's death is acknowledged in the text as the consequence of a natural defensive act toward the offspring, as confirmed by the simile that the author employs, by means of the usual ventriloquist technique, to establish a comparison between the woman and animal mothers who fight tooth and nail for their cubs (46). On a similar note, the denunciation of pedophilic acts is defined by Matilde's character as a feminine duty, because it is to women that "nature entrusted children." (47)

This brief analysis indicates that the reference to clichéd gender roles is supported by the adoption of narrative modes that traditionally belong to the sphere of the literary, which Covella employs with the aim of enhancing her storytelling pathos and with the objective of filling some of the gaps left by documents or testimonies. It is not a coincidence that the majority of essentialist allusions are conveyed by the use of metaphors and similes (as in the cases of Emiliana and Matilde) or by means of Covella's (re)creation of the victim's thoughts (as in the cases of Enza and Matilde). As already noticed in relation to Fiorucci's work, these literary techniques contribute to the stimulation of compassion in the reader, thus enhancing the process of mirroring and guaranteeing a moving denunciation of the phenomenon of femicide. However, they are not enough to trigger the Iserian identification process because of the structural absence of gaps in the plot and more importantly, because of the narrative's incapacity to challenge the reader's horizon of expectation on a moral level.

The tendency in *Fiore… come me* to implement only the most superficial aspects of the metadiscourse on femicide (e.g. the condemnation of lethal gender violence and a clear interest for the figure of the victim) is showcased not only by the text's failure to challenge traditional gender roles, but also by its portrayal of perpetrators as deviant or monstrous Others. Covella dedicates a limited space to the figures of the murderers, thus aligning to the ethos of the victim-centered discourse and highlighting the author's aim to offer a counter-narrative to the journalistic coverage of femicide. However, this alignment proves to be merely superficial if we consider the presence, in the book, of textual occurrences that testify to the volume's reproduction of critical discursive features typically employed in periodical journalism to exclude the perpetrator from the realm of normativity. In two cases, for example, the killer is described as a jealous man (20) who suddenly goes crazy (40), which replicates the frames of romantic love and loss of control that dominate the journalistic coverage of these murder cases (Gius and Lalli 2014:63–66). Similarly, the perpetrators are frequently associated with the category of the nonhuman by means of the employment of labels such as that of monster (Covella 2013:27–28), beast or animal (31;39;94), ogre (31;47), and devil (95). Here, as in the representation of the murdered women, the use of phrases that boost the pathos increases the perception of a polarization between victims and perpetrators, thus contributing to a dichotomous representation of femicide that is even more problematic given the absence of a clear statement on the author's partiality.

Nessuna più, an anthology edited by Marilù Oliva,[1] was published in 2013 by the small but nationally known editor Elliot and it was distributed widely in Italian bookshops. Similar to Covella's work, it resorts to the popular form of the short story. Despite sharing the same literary form and a similar interest in deceiving the annihilating process that femicidal violence imposes on victims by employing the weapon of storytelling, Oliva's text relies on a completely different approach towards journalistic narratives. The forty writers (both women and men) who contributed to the volume took inspiration from true femicide cases covered by the press but erased or changed the names of the protagonists and places, thus making the association between journalistic fact and narrated story difficult. This decision, which corresponds to the publisher's need to avoid potential retaliations (Oliva and Mandolini 2017:225), determines the emancipation of the whole narrative process from the principle of adherence to reality, which is also explicitly addressed by the editor in the following introductory note:

> Some stories, in this book, were freely invented, to the extent that the references to facts should be considered as a simple act of dedication or commemoration. All the rest should be returned to the autonomy of art and the narrated places, events, and persons are the products of the authors' creativity. (Oliva 2013:8)

As this quotation confirms, the anthology's clear literary attitude is determined by the text's ability to free itself from the imperative of verifiability and by the decision to deal with true events deprived of their recognizability. This does not prevent *Nessuna più* from conserving a strict relationship with the practice of journalistic narrative. The readers' inability to identify the short stories' factual referent, in fact, is coupled with a generalized awareness of the narrated stories' nonfictional origin. The productive discontinuity between the singular and the general link to the reality of femicide positions the book as a direct product of the social phenomenon and, at the same time, as a tool that creatively reshapes it.

The introduction openly puts the volume in dialectic dialog with journalistic accounts on lethal gender violence against women by means of frequent mentions to the editor's intention to confront the issues that characterize the press' coverage of femicide. The meta-discourse on the representation of femicide, for example, is indirectly referenced by Oliva, who writes about the need to overcome the justificatory rhetoric implied in the adoption of expressions such as "jealousy outburst" or "crime of passion," (Oliva 2013:7–8) both still present in journalistic reports on women's murders produced in 2012 (Giomi 2015:563; Gius and Lalli 2014:63–66). According to the editor, this rhetoric should be substituted with a clear description of the social and cultural factors that feminists have identified as responsible for the perpetuation of the femicide practice (Oliva 2013:8). Oliva also opposes the anthology's lack of "sensationalizing and pathetic hints" (9) to the spectacularizing attitude that the association Gi.U.Li.A. identified in journalist's femicide chronicles (Betti 2013).

Moreover, (mostly negative) allusions to the sphere of journalistic narratives are not absent in the thirty-eight stories that compose the book. In "Il trillo del diavolo" by Marina Marazza, the textual element of the journalistic article symbolizes both memory and transience, as confirmed by the enigmatic figure of an old and mentally unstable lady who obsessively cuts out old newspaper articles on a specific femicide story and offers them to disinterested passers-by (Oliva 2013:155). In "Al di qua della porta" by Massimo Maugeri, on the other hand, the coverage of a femicide case triggers an empathic reaction through which the protagonist experiences the anxiety for the potential loss of his daughter (163). In "La Santa" by Flavia Piccinini and in "Parole per i codardi" by Matteo Strukul, periodical journalism is portrayed as an objectifying narrative procedure that delivers to the reader an image of the victim as mere "murdered body" (194) or fails to represent the phenomenon of femicide as the product of a widespread sexist culture (230).

The stories included in *Nessuna più* do not offer to the reader a univocal representative perspective on the matter of femicide. On the contrary, they testify to the interest in preserving the principle of heterogeneity that Oliva refers to in the introduction as one of the guiding criteria of the editing process. This results in the proliferation of authorial and narratological points of view: the stories are written by male, female, single and multiple writers; the narrators are either neutral, males or females who play different roles in the story (victims, perpetrators, bystanders, even inanimate objects), or simply act as omniscient tellers. The declared choice to adopt multiple perspectives (8–9) manifests the laudable intention to reproduce the complexity of the phenomenon and its possible representations. However, this decision results in the production of small inconsistencies that risk affecting the volume's overall quality and ethical treatment of femicide. As the analysis on the depiction of the victim that follows will demonstrate, it is possible to identify a general tendency towards a respectful representation of the victims' subjectivity or a propensity to portray the act of lethal violence as the product of a patriarchal culture that legitimizes possessive attitudes, but some pieces do not align to this practice, thus making a coherent thread that brings together all the stories difficult to find.

In line with its general vocation to display variety, *Nessuna più* also presents victim typologies that differ according to age, social background and status, origin, and even sex. This attention to diversity is coupled to a consistent fair treatment for the abused woman's personhood. Seven texts showcase a victim-centered first-person narrative that relies on a realistic approach (these are stories where the woman eventually survives[2] or the narration is interrupted in the moment of the victim's death), on the practice of hybrid realism already identified in *Fiore… come me*, or on fantastic narrative strategies. The victim's experience is generally selected as the focus even by authors who employ the technique of the omniscient narrator, while stories that employ a first-person narrative centered on figures who are external to the violent act are largely based on the point of view of someone who retains an intersubjective link with the victim.

Oliva's anthology generally offers a representation of the victims that successfully transcends traditional gender roles, thus providing an alternative model to the stereotypical portrayal proposed by *Fiore… come me*. In "Dente per dente" by Francesca Bertuzzi, the protagonist, who initially describes herself as "an impotent woman" (Oliva 2013:34) and identifies with the sexist paradigm of the passive victim, progressively emancipates and ends up fantasizing about hypothetical affinities with models of agentic femininity. In particular, before reversing the victim-perpetrator hierarchy and killing her abusive husband with the complicity of her son, the woman describes herself as the popular figure of the Tooth Fairy (36),[3] who she had previously invoked when her abuser slapped her causing the fall of one tooth (33). The intratextual reference to the Tooth Fairy testifies to the symbolic change in the woman's perception of herself and promotes a portrayal of the victim that, despite not avoiding the description of the process of objectification and infantilization determined by violence, highlights the protagonist's capacity of resistance and agency.

The prototype of the passive and weak victim is accurately avoided in almost all of *Nessuna più*'s stories and, if present, it is compensated by the explicit characterization of other female characters as tenacious women. This is the case of "Ciao mamma," a short text inspired by the facts of the aforementioned Circeo massacre where the voice of the woman who survived insists on the weaknesses of her killed friend with the precise aim of affirming her own strength and resilience (201).

This promising tendency in the representation of the victim is confirmed by the fact that the majority of the contributions included in the anthology reject the practice of idealizing the victim on the basis of the patriarchal polarization between good and bad women, which is furtherly amplified by the presence of three stories dedicated to the femicide of sex workers ("Acqua terra aria fuoco" by Francesca Genti; "Lady Lazar" by Lara Manni; "Sara" by Vittoria A).

Only two texts are problematic when it comes to the idealization of the victim. In the aforementioned "Ciao mamma," the victim represents herself as a de-eroticized virginal subject (201) and it is precisely on this assumption that she frames her innocence and the accusation of the perpetrators (204). In "Ancora una volta il tuo respiro" by Cristina Zagaria, the mother of a femicide victim describes her daughter as a girl who "played the woman" but who "only kissed her boyfriend on his cheeks," (246) so as to convey an idea of purity that reinforces the idea of victimhood.

The trope of maternity, which is exploited in *Fiore… come me* and supports a stereotypical depiction of the murdered woman, is present in many of *Nessuna più*'s stories: in some cases, love for their children sustains some of the portrayed victims of abuse in their survival path; in other cases, the condition of pregnancy is underlined by the authors with the aim of giving an account of the supplementary ferocity that characterizes the abusive acts. However, the recursivity of the maternity trope does not result, as it does in Covella's work, in the reproduction of the essentialist paradigm according to which motherly cure is a propensity inherently linked to female subjects. This is demonstrated by the inclusion in the anthology of short stories such as "Non sarà mai l'ultima" by

Piergiorgio Pulixi and "Mia è la vendetta" by Gaja Cenciarelli, where abusive mothers or mothers who indirectly participate in the violence inflicted on gender violence victims are portrayed.

Nessuna più manifests a general, though not absolute, tendency to align with the guidelines on the representation of femicide victims provided by feminist metadiscourse. The same can be said about the portrayal of perpetrators, which clearly exhibits consistency with the editor's introductory statements on the rejection of discursive strategies aimed at diminishing the murderer's responsibility. If we exclude the short story "Stalker" by Raul Montanari, where the killer's first-person narrative reproduces the journalistic frame of the loss of control and does not contribute to the denunciation of the man's possessive behavior, other texts describe and challenge the justificatory rhetoric that supports the perpetrator's actions, even when they are centered on the murderer's point of view. In "Io l'amavo…," Marco Vichi employs the narrative technique of the dialog to contest the killer's declarations through the voice of the policemen who interrogates him (231–236). In "Gentile," Lorenzo Ghinelli's decision to juxtapose the perpetrator and victim's narratives and to position the man's statements after the woman's, assigns discursive preference to the accusation of guilt vocalized by the abused (113–116). In "Mia" by Fabrizio Lorusso, the murderer self-criticizes himself by deconstructing his own justifications: "It was a deliberate act, not an outburst. Revenge, this is me"; (131) "Her fault? No, I did it on my own." (133)

Notwithstanding the presence of some positive details, Oliva's volume is not devoid of problematic elements when it comes to the depiction of those who exercise violence. The propensity to provide a simplistic portrayal of the perpetrator, which is often coupled with the use of labels that inscribe him in the realm of deviancy, testifies to the previously discussed pitfalls of the rigidly victim-centered discourse. In short-stories such as "Dente per dente," "Lettera a Laura" by Milva Comastri, "Il tempo di un bacio" by Laura Liberale, "Lady Lazar," "Sara," and "Non sarà mai l'ultima," the victim-centered perspective does not leave further space for a structured representation of the male character. Moreover, some texts resort to epithets that label perpetrators as monstrous ("Guardami" by Sara Bilotti and "Bruciata viva" by Mariangela Camocardi) or mentally unstable ("Satana nella zona giorno" by Alessandro Berselli, "Guardami," "Le voci dal muro" by Maurizio de Giovanni, "Non tutti nella capitale sbocciano i fiori del male" by Alessia Gazzola, "Lady Lazar"), which conceals the cultural dynamics that characterize gender violence. This very tendency is reproduced even in the preface drafted by the criminologist Roberta

Bruzzone, who uses the expression "ogres next-door" (17) to identify those who commit femicide.

In *Nessuna più*, texts that provide this overly simplified image of perpetrators are juxtaposed with texts that contribute to the development of feminist discourse on femicide with a fair representation of the murderers and a refined reflection on the psycho-social construction of masculinity. In "Fuoco amico" by Laura Costantini and Loredana Falcone, the omniscient narrator clearly delineates the perpetrator's possessive attitude as well as his desire for omnipotence, which is conveyed by the use of capital letters in the transcription of pronouns referred to him. Furthermore, the typical femicidal man's tendency to confuse his partner's role with that of a mother, and consequently demand exclusive care from her side (Melandri 2011: 98), is disclosed in the passage that follows:

> And the fire will be her punishment. Because she ceased to be as He created her. Because she mocked His manias. Because she deprived Him of everything that made of Him a man. The wife, the house, the kids that He didn't want. The kids who forced Him out of the realm of her attentions. (66)

Another significant contribution to feminist discourse on lethal gender violence is the presence, in some of the short stories in *Nessuna più*, of narrative elements that trouble the binary paradigm that dominates discussions on violence against women, namely the division between victims belonging to the female sex and male perpetrators. This is made possible by the decision of representing transsexual victims ("Princesa" by Stefano Caso) and women who contribute to the implementation of the patriarchal abusive dynamics (the *maman* who controls the prostitution market in "Acqua terra aria fuoco"[4] and the complicit mothers of "Bruciata viva" and "Non sarà mai l'ultima").

Coherently following Oliva's direct critique of spectacularization and sensationalism, *Nessuna più* exhibits a clear effort to propose alternative solutions to the re-objectifying exposure of bodies annihilated by violence. This effort is generally associated with the employment of hybrid realism or fantastic narrative techniques. In "La forma di ciò che sono" by Marco Marsullo, the first-person narrative is carried out by the knife used by the perpetrator for the femicide of a girl. The knife fantastically reflects on its involuntary action while entering the victim's flesh, which determines a microscopic effect that, through the combination of realistic and fantastic elements, allows the author to avoid the reproduction of images of reified femininity. As a result, the murdered girl is depicted only in the moment that precedes the assault, when the killer lifts the knife and the object can see and describe her while she is alive, a desiring subject: "From my position I could see the girl, I could meet her gaze, I could read her memories. From my position, she seemed even smaller. Small, with the desire to experience a different world." (159–160)

In a similar manner "Io sono la Chiesa" by Marilù Oliva, resorts to hybrid realism to create the impression of a macroscopic perspective centered on the inanimate object of the church where the body of the victim was found. Focusing on the church's material aspect and depriving it of any symbolic components (its spiritual and institutional dimension), Oliva's adoption of the unusual narratological point of view of the building permits to interrupt the description of the events just a moment before the femicide, with an image that immortalizes the young woman when alive (2013:188). The graphic representation of the abuse is substituted by the reflections of the church/narrator, who discharges itself from the responsibility of reporting the "unprecedented abuses" because its testimony, which is articulated from an eccentric angle, has no legitimacy in front of the law (188–189).

A further demonstration of the productivity of hybrid realism for the creation of non-objectifying representations of gender violence is provided by Wu Ming 1, who identified the technique of assigning narratological relevance to eccentric/marginalized subjects or to inanimate objects in many literary texts published in Italy since the second part of the Nineties. This oblique gaze is defined by Wu Ming 1 as "the exploration of unexpected and uncommon points of view including those of animals, objects, places or even immaterial fluxes" (2009:26) and it is addressed as a fruitful formal strategy for overcoming the perspective rigidity that sustains the cultural construction of normativity (81). This easily applies to the effort of challenging dominant re-objectifying practices that characterize feminist representations of femicide such as the short stories in *Nessuna più*, where the adoption of an eccentric narrator upsets the rigor of the opposition between male narrating subject and female narrated object that distinguishes patriarchal discourse.

If we exclude Marsullo and Oliva's stories, portrayals of the violated female body and graphic scenes of abuse are present in the anthology. In the majority of cases, however, these depictions are included in texts where the narratological perspective coincides with that of the victim, which testifies to the choice of using the images to condemn brutality only where this practice does not jeopardize the representation of female figures as agentive subjects. For example, in "Acqua terra aria fuoco" and "Pensieri sull'acqua" by Andrea Novelli and Giampaolo Zarini, the torments suffered by the woman and the image of her corpse are presented by a first-person narrative carried out by the deceased victim through which the authors overcome the boundaries imposed by death and use the graphic depiction as a strategy of denunciation.

In *Nessuna più*, the rejection of spectacularization[5] is paired with the clear effort to provide readers with stories that trigger a process of mirroring and/or identification. Mirroring is promoted by the frequent adoption of an intersubjective dynamic which is often associated with the female characters. In "La Santa," for example, the woman journalist who acts as protagonist unveils the story of Maria – the fictional name that substitutes Lea Garofalo, a cooperating witness who was killed on the order of her mobster ex-husband – and establishes an emotional connection with it. References to the idea of sisterhood are reiterated in the text (198;199) and they are further confirmed by the association between Maria's tragedy and that of the journalist's guide, who is implicitly referenced as a survivor of patriarchal violence. In cases such as this, the presence of an intersubjective network that connects female characters cannot but generate a process of mirroring or empathy in female readers, who are likely to perceive themselves as belonging to the represented relational dynamics.

Female-based intersubjectivity is also present in "Princesa," where the narrator-protagonist discovers that her husband cheated on her with Patty, a transsexual prostitute who was killed by unknown assailants. Following the disclosure of the adultery, the protagonist decides to seek revenge and she chases her partner in her car, with the objective of killing him in a lethal accident. However, she accidentally drives off the road and slips into a coma. Here, the use of hybrid realism permits the vocalization of the comatose woman's condemnation of patriarchal culture as well as of her posthumous identification with the character of Patty. The connection between the two potentially rival women is established on the basis of the recognition of a common destiny of oppression that, in both cases, resulted in physical and/or mental annihilation. This affinity is confirmed by the name that the protagonist imagines for the baby she lost during the accident: "Valchiria Addolorata" [Grieving Valkyrie], which encloses the ideas of "fierceness" and "pain" (50;53) that are recognized as characteristics of Patty as well as of "all victims of femicide." (53) The fact that, in "Princesa," female intersubjectivity refers to the relationship with a transsexual woman and that the symbolic attributes associated with an MtF (Male-to-Female) transsexual subject correlate to those assigned to gender abuse victims, profitably troubles the hetero-cis-normative standard that often informs discourses on violence against women. In this sense, the reader's horizon of expectations is fruitfully deluded.

The thematic break with the receiver's supposed ethical prospect is accompanied by the presence of a significant lack of definition in the plot, which is determined by the unknown identity of Patty's killer. This structural gap, which stimulates the reader's participation in the creation of meaning and guarantees the openness of the text, is made possible by the authors' freedom of approach to the original factual material. Building a clearly fictional narrative on the reality of the unresolved femicide, Caso vaguely adumbrates the protagonist's husband's involvement in the crime by portraying him while he vocalizes transphobic insults and describes an episode of sexual violence committed against Patty to friends. Apart from suggesting the conceptual tie between milder gender discriminations and femicide, this narratological strategy accentuates the atmosphere of uncertainty, thus encouraging that active reading process that Iser observed as crucial for identification.

Like "Princesa," other short stories included in *Nessuna più* demonstrate that textual openness results from an explicitly fictional approach to the narrative process. This is also the case of "La Santa," where intersubjectivity is complemented by the presence of narrative omissions that would not be acceptable in a text aimed at providing the reader with a documented and verifiable account of real events. In "La Santa," this is confirmed by the ambiguity that concerns the character of the journalist's guide and her evoked, though never confirmed, past experience as a domestic violence victim. It is precisely on the presence of a non-homogenous but significant degree of openness that *Nessuna più* ultimately differs from *Fiore… come me*, where a similar mission and form produce antithetical results given the narrative's position of pseudo-objectivity, which does not support textual omissions and ambiguities.

Notes

1 Oliva is a renewed writer in the context of Italian crime literature. Among other novels, she published *¡Tú la pagarás!* (2010), *Fuego* (2011), *Mala Suerte* (2012), *Le sultane* (2014). On the topic of femicide, she wrote *Le spose sepolte* (2018).

2 The woman's survival does not prevent us to label the represented act as femicide if, as in the cases portrayed in *Nessuna più*, the victim undergoes a psychological and physical annihilation that coincides with the idea of "living death" introduced by Nadera Shalhoub-Kevorkian while describing the prolonged abused suffered by women who are condemned to the practice of honor killing (2003).

3 The Tooth Fairy is a figure of Western popular tradition that is commonly awaited by children when they lose their baby teeth. As the story goes, if the lost tooth is placed under the pillow, she will replace it with a gift (usually money).
4 In the context of Nigerian sex trafficking in Italy, the *maman* is the female figure, an ex-prostitute herself, who controls the prostitution business and profits from it. On this, see Lo Iacono (2014).
5 There are only two of the short stories where the victim's body is re-objectified, which once again demonstrates the heterogeneity of the anthology. In "Qualcuno di troppo in famiglia" by Loriano Macchiavelli, the woman is seen through the male protagonist's gaze and she is described as the object of his sexual interest, even after the rape she suffers: "Her petticoat was untied up until the breast, her legs were open and red for her virginal blood and for the blood coming from the many cuts she had on the abdomen and on the breasts." (143) Similarly, in "Non sarà mai l'ultima," the corpse of the victim is eroticized and presented as a "macabre ebony statue" with "the cunt open and red as a broken watermelon" (206).

Works cited

Benedict, H. (1992) *Virgin or Vamp. How the Press Covers Sex Crimes*. Cambridge, Massachusetts, and London: Harvard University Press.

Bennett, A. (2012) *Afterlife and Narrative in Contemporary Fiction*. New York: Palgrave.

Betti, L. (2013) Il #25 novembre dura fino al 10 dicembre. *Giuliaglobalist*. November 30: https://www.globalist.it/media/2016/05/08/il-25-novembre-dura-fino-al-10-dicembre-51909.html. Accessed 22 November 2020.

Binik, O. (2015) "Ideali e meritevoli: le donne vittime di femicidio nel dibattito pubblico in Italia. Uno studio sulla trasmissione *Quarto Grado*," *Studi culturali*3:391–412.

Christie, N. (1986) "The Ideal Victim," in Fattaj, E. A. (ed.), *From Crime Policy to Victim Policy. Reorienting the Justice System*. New York: Palgrave, pp. 17–30.

Covella, G. (2013) *Fiore... come me. Storie di dieci vite spezzate*. Naples: Spazio Creativo.

Ercolino, S. (2015) *Il romanzo massimalista*. Milan: Bompiani.

Fine, M. and Asch, A. (1981) "Disabled Women: Sexism without the Pedestal," *Journal of Sociology & Social Welfare* 8:233.

Giomi, E. (2015) "Tag femminicidio. La violenza letale contro le donne nella stampa italiana," *Problemi dell'informazione* 50(3):549–574.

Gius, C. and Lalli, P. (2014) "'I Loved Her So Much, but I Killed Her.' Romantic Love as a Representational Frame for Intimate Partner Femicide in Three Italian Newspapers," *Journal for Communication Studies* 7(2):53–75.

Greer, C. (2007) "News Media, Victims and Crime," in Davies, P., Francis, P. and Greer, C. (eds.), *Victims, Crime and Society*. Los Angeles, London, New Delhi, Singapore: Sage, pp. 20–49.

Lo Iacono, E. (2014) "Victims, Sex Workers and Perpetrators: Gray Areas in the Trafficking of Nigerian Women," *Trends in Organized Crime* 17(1–2):110–128.

Melandri, L. (2011). *Amore e violenza. Il fattore molesto della civiltà.* Turin: Bollati Boringhieri.

Oliva, M. (ed.) (2013) *Nessuna più. Quaranta scrittori contro il femminicidio*. Rome: Elliot.

Oliva, M. (2010) *¡Tú la pagarás!*. Rome: Elliot.

Oliva, M. (2011) *Fuego*. Rome: Elliot.

Oliva, M. (2012) *Mala suerte*. Rome: Elliot.

Oliva, M. (2014) *Le sultane*. Rome: Elliot.

Oliva, M. (2018) *Le spose sepolte*. Milan: Harper Collins.

Oliva, M. and Mandolini, N. (2017) "Una femminista in incognito contro il femminicidio. Intervista a Marilù Oliva," *gender/sexuality/italy* 4:217–230: https://www.gendersexualityitaly.com/wp-content/uploads/2017/09/25.-Mandolini-Una-Femminista-in-Incognito-2.pdf Accessed 14 November 2020.

Pickering-Iazzi, R. (2018) "Il femminicidio e il genere nella biografia testimoniale come pratica sociale e simbolica," in Bettaglio, M., Mandolini, N. and Ross, S. (eds.), *Rappresentare la violenza di genere. Sguardi femministi tra critica, attivismo e scrittura*. Milan: Mimesis, pp. 71–92.

Siani, P. (2013) "Introduzione," in Covella, G. (ed.) *Fiore... come me*. Naples: Spazio Creativo, pp. 11–14.

Shalhoub-Kevorkian, N. (2003) "Reexamining Femicide: Breaking the Silence and Crossing 'Scientific' Borders," *Signs* 28(2):581–608.

Thomson, R. G. (1997) "Feminist Theory, the Body, and the Disabled Figure," in Davis, L. J. (ed.) *The Disability Studies Reader*. New York and London: Routledge, pp. 279–294.

7 Rewriting history: *La scuola cattolica* (2016) by Edoardo Albinati

La scuola cattolica by Edoardo Albinati[1] entered the national literary context in 2016.[2] Notwithstanding the positive responses of literary critics, which led to the award of the most prestigious book prize in Italy, the Premio Strega, *La scuola cattolica* has received some negative reviews from readers who blamed the text for its excessive length (it is 1294 pages long in the original Italian version) and for its frequent repetitions (Gasperina Geroni 2018a:128). For this reason, Albinati's work differs from *Fiore… come me* and *Nessuna più*, both books in the short-story format that appeal to the modern reader's inclination to consume multiple and brief narratives.[3] The lack of attractiveness of the lengthy format originates from the author's need to engage in an exploration of his self by means of a prolonged memorial effort and reflection, which can be supported only by a dilated narrative structure (Gasperina Geroni 2018a:128). In light of this, the novel can be described as a long rumination accompanied by narrative digressions that the protagonist-narrator (Albinati's autofictional alter-ego) conducts in relation to his own formation at the Roman religious school San Leone Magno, where, during the Seventies, the author was a schoolmate of Angelo Izzo, Gianni Guido, and Andrea Ghira, the perpetrators of the Circeo massacre. As already noted by critics who analyzed the text, the historical events of the Circeo massacre are the novel's "empty" heart (Gasperina Geroni 2018b:109), to which the narrative tends and from which it constantly departs in order to find space for meditations and stories on connected topics, such as the relationship between males and females or the classist and gendered violence that characterized the decade of the Seventies in Italy (Cortellessa 2016; Savettieri 2018:126).

More information on the book can be deduced from the statements released by the author, who dates the beginning of the writing process to 2005, when Angelo Izzo committed a second femicide, killing Maria

DOI: 10.4324/9781003120339-7

Carmela Limucciano and Valentina Maiorano during a short period outside of the penitentiary where he was jailed for the crimes of the Circeo massacre (Albinati 2016b:51). According to Albinati, the re-actualization in the realm of contemporary events of the massacre carried out in the Seventies determined the desire to undertake a cathartic renarration of the events, in which he participated as indirect witness (Albinati 2016b:51). In light of this, the centrality of the double femicidal event is clear. However, the author decides to approximate it by means of a vertical movement of personal scrutiny and storytelling, as opposed to a horizontal description of facts that cannot be known because they were not directly experienced. As a result, the historical event is rewritten by means of an implicit moral association between the behaviors and the beliefs of the narrating self and those of the perpetrators (Izzo, in particular). This concordance is guaranteed by their common position as upper-middle-class males and it is symbolically confirmed by the spatial and temporal contiguity that determined an overlap of their life paths at the San Leone Magno and in the Roman neighborhood Trieste, where they all lived at the time of the massacre. Albinati explained his choices writing:

> First of all, my own recognition as male and the practice of starting from myself connected me or, so to speak, resonated with the obscure part of masculinity, which is represented precisely by those murderers that I met at school. (2016b:51)

The expression "starting from myself" (*partire da me*, in Italian) used by Albinati to describe the personal interrogation that initiated the writing process is borrowed from feminist discourse. It is not a coincidence that in the 1970s, Italian feminist movements imported from the United States the idea of consciousness raising, a political practice that provided feminists with the tools to elaborate a critique of the dynamics of patriarchal domination through the analysis of the private experiences of oppression lived by the women who participated in it. Consciousness raising (*autocoscienza*, in the Italian context)[4] comprised of the creation of small groups of women who gathered periodically to discuss their gender positioning and confront on personal matters. The feminist motto the personal is political, which in Italy was translated into the recommendation *partire da sé* [to start from oneself] when enacting feminist politics, originated from this activist practice. The imperative of *partire da sé* to which Albinati makes reference permitted to consciousness raising groups not only to verify the incidence of sexism in the realm of personal and political relationships but also fostered the development of a female subjectivity by supporting the act of self-narration. As the Italian feminist activist Lia Cigarini noted, the idea of partiality or positioning of the gendered point of view from which the practice of *partire da sé*/*autocoscienza* stems was used to overcome the male-centered and universalizing rhetoric of patriarchal discourse as well as to promote female authority/authoriality with the aim of imagining a more equal society by establishing difference as a guiding principle (1995:146–147).

The novel's structure substantiates the link with the experience of consciousness raising. The reflexive mode that characterizes the narrative recalls the practice of internal scrutiny that defined the *autocoscienza* meetings, while the frequent digressions through which the narrator openly converses with the reader and the inclusion in the text of stories told by male-gendered subjects with whom the protagonist relates re-create the intersubjective narrative dynamic that was crucial to the feminist sessions. Notwithstanding this effort, the consciousness raising operation carried out by *La scuola cattolica*'s narrator does not completely overlap with that conducted by feminist activists. This has very much to do with the male gender positioning from which the protagonist-narrator explicitly conducts his authorial enterprise. In order to maintain unchanged feminist consciousness raising's objective of challenging the subordination of women, a male-centered *partire da sé* should aim at describing and criticizing the authoritarian model imposed by hegemonic masculinity. In other words, it should work for the de-construction (as opposed to the construction that applies to the case of women) of its authorial voice. As stated by Warren Thomas Farrell, the rare phenomenon of male-based consciousness raising is an attempt carried out by subjects belonging to a socially dominant category to acquire awareness on their privilege so as to subsequently abolish it (1972). The following analysis will demonstrate how it is precisely on the inversion of the traditional dynamics of feminist consciousness raising that lies the peculiarity of Albinati's rewriting of the Circeo events.

The choice of autofiction perfectly fits the project of revising feminist consciousness raising from a male perspective. Used for the first time by the French writer Serge Doubrovsky to label his hybrid autobiography *Fils* (1977), autofiction is a writing form in which the names of the author and that of the protagonist-narrator overlap. However, autofiction differs from autobiography for the presence of paratextual or textual elements that encourage the reader to doubt the narrative's factuality. In other words, in autofictional texts, the author manifests the intent of "provoking an attrite between reality and novelistic invention." (Marchese 2014: 186)

La scuola cattolica's autofictional dimension is determined by the typology of pact that the author establishes with the receiver. On the basis of a paratextual note where the novel is presented as a mixture of real events and imagined situations, the reader experiences an "interpretative disorientation" that leaves no choice but to embrace the ambiguity that the work invites (Gasperina Geroni 2018b:111–112). Notwithstanding the presence of a close relationship with the events, which amplifies the work's capacity of denouncing the phenomenon of gender violence, Albinati's narration instills a persistent doubt in the receiver of the tale's truthful value, which contributes to connote the narrator as unreliable (Booth 1983:211-364). This unreliability is evoked by the narrator's recurring statements on the fallacy of his memory and on the need to compensate it with fictional accounts (Albinati 2019:III.17;IV.20;V.1;VIII.15;X.7) or with a combination of facts and fiction (II.9;III.11;III.15;V.8;VII.18). In this sense, Albinati constructs his work respecting one of the constitutive traits of autofiction: the erosion of the author-protagonist's subjectivity and authoriality (Marchese 2014:265). Therefore, autofiction is a form that allows the writer to give an account of himself and of his complicity with the dynamics of patriarchal domination. Moreover, autofiction permits the male author to undermine his authorial hegemony with the objective of leveling the gender hierarchy and working toward the de-objectification of the feminine.

The clear references to the form of autofiction do not prevent *La scuola cattolica* from offering allusions to other literary genres such as that of the historical novel. The urgency of narrating the self acquires consistency in relation to a broader need to renarrate historical events that, as in the cases of the previously mentioned *La Storia* and *Artemisia*, were relegated to the margins by patriarchal historiography. It is not a coincidence that Albinati rewrites the Circeo massacre and the thrilling political season of the Seventies by assigning a renewed centrality to gender issues, which were previously concealed by a narration of the events centered on more eminently political topics such as class discrimination (Gasperina Geroni 2018b:117–120). However, the novel differs from Morante and Banti's works because the need to deconstruct sexist historical narratives cannot but manifest itself as a critical relationship of the narrator – who is consciously positioned as a man – to his own discourse. Herein lies the reason of the narrator's conflictual relationship with the idea of memory, the concept around which *Artemisia* and the other of the journalistic and literary texts on femicide analyzed so far are constructed.

On one side, the protagonist tells and analyzes the social and cultural mechanisms that produced the hegemony of abusive masculinity in the past as well as in the present.[5] On the other, he portrays his storytelling practice as a process that aims at catharsis, as opposed to memorial conservation, and he invites the receiver to consider what he is reading as a burial of the authorial voice: "I write not to remember this story, on the contrary, I write so it could be sealed and forgotten forever. At least from my side. I close the story inside this book as if I'd bury it." (Albinati 2019:VIII.15) This oscillating movement, which combines a descriptive approach and a critical tendency, also characterizes the novel at a thematic level. In this regard, Cristina Savettieri labeled Albinati's work as discontinuous and inconsistent, especially when it comes to the topic of violence against women (2017:129–134). The fluctuating and often contradictory nature of the narrating voice's opinion is demonstrated by the frequent juxtaposition of a denunciation of the psychosocial dynamics that lead to gender violence with a stereotyping rhetoric that produces objectifying and essentializing representations of the feminine. Between chapter IV and VI of the second part of *La scuola cattolica*, for example, the narrator embarks on a long reflection on what distinguishes men from women and he implicitly references Raewyn Connell's theories on hegemonic masculinity[6] when he admits that gender categories are socially constructed (II.4). However, the culturalist feminist approach is subsequently eroded by essentialist statements that portray the woman as a subject who is naturally devoted to motherhood (II.5). The same feminist approach is then reiterated at the beginning of the following chapter when, with another U-turn, the protagonist blames thinkers who resort to hypothetical natural laws to justify sexist violence (II.6).

This ambiguous discourse on pressing social issues such as gender abuse is undeniably problematic. Nonetheless, the position of the narrator as an equivocal figure who vacillates between antithetical ideological standpoints (Bonfili 2016:278) is not completely unfavorable if we consider the contribution that this narratological practice brings to the process of de-structuration of the authorial reliability. This is coupled with the deconstruction of the dominant model of masculinity, which, despite being described and discursively confirmed by the narrator, is constantly subjected to a dissection that ultimately unveils the rhetorical processes that legitimize abusive behaviors and speech.

The aforementioned dynamic characterizes many passages of *La scuola cattolica*. Among these, an insert to chapter I and II of the sixth part, where the narrator makes direct reference to the storytelling performed by Max, a young fascist the teenager protagonist meets during his summer holidays in Tuscany. Max's narrative is aimed at describing his participation in the left-wing Festival of Parco Lambro (1974), one of the first gatherings where Italian youths experienced drugs and sexual liberation. Max's eye-popping confessions about his sexual encounters with young women who took part in the event are welcomed by the narrator, who defines his companion as a crusader who "had ventured into enemy territory to fuck the infidel wenches." (Albinati 2019:VI.1) However, just a few pages after, Max's tale is labeled as deceitful in light of a check carried out by the narrator on a filmic document in which there was no sign "of the alluring sirens that Max claimed he had fucked." (VI.1) Here, the narrator starts with a praise of Max's anecdote, which he reads as an attestation of virility, but he ends up revealing the mendacity of his friend's narrative, thus unmasking his secret homosocial intention to impress. By means of this oscillatory account, Albinati displays the unreliability of male-authored storytelling as well as the objectification of female corporality and subjectivity, which is clearly used by Max as a rhetorical device aimed at fostering male bonding.[7]

The alternation between a deconstructive and a conservative perspective sheds light on the dialog that *La scuola cattolica*'s protagonist establishes with feminist theories, as well as on his incapacity of implementing these theories at a discursive and behavioral level. In other words, the narrating voice appears as a subject who attempts at challenging his gender privilege and, at the same time, as an individual who is fully compromised with patriarchal practices, the same practices from which the perpetrators of the Circeo massacre took the first step toward performing their violent deeds. The moral nexus with the mentality that legitimizes gender violence is confirmed by the behavior of the protagonist toward Bettina, a young woman who, during a sexual act, explicitly expresses her erotic desire. The narrator retaliates against her initiative by practicing anal sex on her, which leaves Bettina inert and devoid of agency, as stated in the anecdote's conclusive sentence: "Her buttocks gleamed white in the darkness, and she seemed dead, she wasn't moving, she no longer seemed to be breathing." (VII.18)

Albinati's novel selects male receivers who conform to the heterosexual norm – that is to say, the identitary type that statistically corresponds to the profile of the abusing subject (Goldner et al. 1990; Anderson and Umberson 2001; FRA 2014:27) – as its implied readers. It is precisely for this reason that the novel's ethical value is not only ascribable to the deconstruction of male literary authoriality. On the contrary, *La scuola cattolica*'s autofiction also guides the reader toward a disorientation that facilitates the development of a new awareness and consequently upsets the toughness of assimilated patriarchal values. This process starts from the stimulation of the receivers' sense of complicity with the figure of the narrator and by extension, with the perpetrators of the Circeo massacre by means of a storytelling practice that insists on anecdotes that reproduce common homosocial dynamics and typical tendencies of male teenage behavior. The inconvenient connection with deplorable individuals, where this threefold game of mirrors leads, is required in order to foster the readers' level of consciousness on their gender privilege as well as on the systematic and widespread practice of objectifying women. The oscillatory movement that characterizes Albinati's narrative does not allow those who read to stop at the phase of recognition and induces in the recipient a reflexive process that problematizes the supposed naturalness of gender hierarchy, thus avoiding any justificatory attitude. In particular, the reader seesaws, following the narrator's vacillations, between the familiar (the identification with the system of patriarchal values) and the non-familiar (the critique of the same system). To phrase this using Umberto Eco's theories, the receiver is asked to undertake "inferential walks" during which he provisionally moves away from the text and appeals to what he already knows, to the "repertoire of the already said." But when he goes back to reading, his inference based on common sense (his horizon of expectations, to use Jauss' terminology) is dismissed and his preset moral framework is disassembled (Eco 1979:118).

Notwithstanding the ethical and political merits of fluctuating storytelling, the deconstruction of male authority and authoriality is only partially accomplished if we consider that, for the course of almost all the book, women are not only described as subordinated, they are also consistently silenced (Raimo 2016). If male characters are allowed full space in the narrator's discourse – a space that hosts the deconstruction of patriarchal rhetorical devices, but a space, still – female figures are generally addressed as narrative objects. The propensity to deprive women of their own voice and subjectivity is even noticed by the narrator, who confesses his reifying thinking toward the most important female character of the novel, his friend's sister, Leda: "In fact, I never find myself thinking about what *she* did, but only about what other people *did to* her…The verbs that have Leda as their subject in my mind are all conjugated in the passive form." (Albinati 2019:VIII.7) The role of the feminine in the text is conceptually associated to that of the silenced and passive victim whose voice the male narrator is unable to reach because of his antithetical gender positioning and because he is deeply aligned with the sexist belief according to which nonerotic approximations toward the feminine would diminish men's degree of virility (VII.8). It is for this reason that, Rosaria Lopez and Donatella Colasanti (the victims of the Circeo massacre) are even deprived of their name, which is substituted by the initials (R.L. and D.C.), while Carmela Limucciano and Valentina Maiorano (the women killed by Izzo in 2005) are barely mentioned.

Only in the conclusive parts of *La scuola cattolica* does the narrator overcome the obliteration of female subjectivity and dismisses the gendered symbolic apparatus upon which the rest of the book is shaped: the opposition between man-perpetrator-author and woman-victim-object of discourse. This is facilitated by the presence of two narrative segments that complement the reflection on the issue of the Circeo crimes.

The first is the re-narration of the murder of Cassio Majuri, a member of the criminal fascist gang to which the Circeo killers belonged. An account of the same event had been already provided by Albinati in the middle of the book, when he transcribed the minutes of Izzo's statements on the illegal activities carried out by the group (VI.14). Majuri's assassination consisted of an act of retaliation against the man's disloyal behavior toward the gang and it involved the solicitation of a young woman who was offered as sexual allurement for the victim. As soon as the woman – who is named Perdìta, like William Shakespeare's protagonist in *The Winter's Tale*, because her name was not included in the minutes with Izzo's declarations – entered the room, Majuri was executed. If the first account of Majuri's killing was authored by Izzo, who occupied the role of perpetrator in the retaliation, in the second version of the story the narrator's voice is complemented by the perspective of Perdìta, "an abused young girl pretending to want to abuse in her turn," (X.12) and by that of Majuri himself, the potential abuser who ended up playing the part of the victim. The shift of the point of view on victimized individuals is confirmed, in the following chapter, by the revelation that the woman involved in Majuri's murder was Arbus' sister, Leda, the victim who now has a name and a renovated subjectivity. This disclosure also allows the narrator to recognize Leda as "the only point that could stitch together all the others in the constellation of her brother's account," (X.12) thus assigning to the female character the central role of discourse pivot.

If the interlude on Majuri's case opens up the protagonist to a new empathy with a victimized female character and, consequently, deconstructs the monadic authoriality of male-based tale, the novel's last two chapters propose an even more direct assonance between the narrator and the ideas of femininity and victimhood. While he is participating in the Christmas mass organized by the San Leone Magno, the protagonist recalls a school trip to the Dolomites during which he fell sick and was assisted by a priest, Father Marenzio. When it comes to the description of the physical proximity between him and the priest, the narrator troubles, for the first time in the whole book, the comprehensiveness of his habitual writing style and employs a non-linear narrative characterized by omissions and oneiric overlapping of temporal planes:

> We rested in the shade of a room with the shatters pulled to, the sun had bronzed us and wearied us, and our games had exhausted us, the sheets were white and cool…the sweat on my forehead dried off on the fabric of Father Marenzio's tunic. […] The serpent breathed in shadows and a naked woman listened to him, then followed him. "Eat this apple. There's nothing wrong with doing it." There's nothing wrong…there's nothing wrong…and she obeyed him. I felt every bit as obedient. It took no effort to obtain my obedience. […] "What a handsome boy you are…" said Father Marenzio, caressing me. "You really are beautiful…" and I could see his face close to mine. […] I fell asleep for a while and then woke back up. The great big angel standing at heaven's gate held a flaming sword, but instead of turning people away, he was waving them in with his sword. I drew close, full of curiosity, even if the light that poured out of the gate, and from the sword, and from the angel, was blinding me. But I still wanted to enter. "Wait, wait." Father Marenzio rubbed his face and his eyes behind the lenses, "Wait," he said, panting, "wait!" and when he started caressing my face and neck again, I felt his large hand was wet. (X .16)

Here, religious symbolism is used to compensate the frequent memory gaps, as well as the absence of clarity and the hallucinated perspective that connote the insert, which evokes the writing approach usually adopted to reconstruct repressed traumatic events.[8] The hypothesis of a sexual abuse experienced during childhood is never explicitly stated in the text, but it is suggested by the phallic connotation of the symbols (the serpent and the sword), by the declared propensity of the narrator to obey, by Father Marenzio's compliments, and by the portrayal of him as panting.

Notwithstanding the intentional ambiguity of the events, the protagonist occupies a clear passive position that aligns him with the perspective of the woman – Eve, who obeys the serpent's orders – and, as never happened before, with that of the victim. This process of feminization is supported by the image of the protagonist's physical contact with a man and by the linked idea of a homosexual encounter, which patriarchal virilist rhetoric commonly considers undermining masculinity. It is not a coincidence that, in the book's conclusive chapter, the protagonist admits to himself: "Perdìta was me, I was Perdìta," (Albinati 2019:X.17) so as to attest to the overcoming of the opposition between the self and the category of victimized femininity, which is now recognized as constitutive of the deconstructed male subjectivity.

The protagonist's new awareness of the presence of a victimized component that breaks his virile integrity and invalidates the possibility of a coherent adhesion to the model of hegemonic masculinity is the result of a storytelling practice that welcomes doubt and lack of definition as its guiding principles. As confirmed by the narrator's own words: "We ought to work more on uncertainty, turn it to our favor, that's right, work for uncertain results." (X:17) Doubt is here the new moral core of a self that abandons its previous rigidity, questions himself and his discourse's adherence to the patriarchal *doxa*, thus provisionally concluding his consciousness raising process.

As the analysis demonstrated, the testimonial method provided by the literary form of the autofiction problematizes *La scuola cattolica*'s relationship with the idea of truth. But at the same time, it supports the production of a narrative that, instead of completely relying on fiction, dialogs with the principle of authenticity by means of the narrator's explicit positioning as a male subject who indirectly participated in the events of the Circeo massacre. The reader's mirroring, which mainly involves heteronormative men who can empathize with the narrator's account of gendered dynamics is also based on this very positioning. In this sense, Albinati's approach possesses an undeniable political value as it triggers an association between the male receiver and the figures of perpetrators of sexist violence by implicitly asking the reader to admit his complicity with the patriarchal order from which abuse stems. The male reader's implied affiliation to the mechanisms of sexist perpetration, however, does not prevent the protagonist from engaging the receiver in the same process of approximation to the position of the victim that, at the end of the novel, he himself undertakes. This is made possible by the act of declaring the reader's inevitable experience of suffering in relation to the narrator's excruciating and enigmatic storytelling practice, which is clearly expressed in the following passage:

> The reader – who if he is of the male gender might or ought to identify with the various monsignors and gentlemen, and take pleasure alongside them in their erotic misdeeds – instead finds

> himself in a position similar to that of the young girls who have been abused: he undergoes unbroken violence and so he learns. (VII.13)

Despite its political value, the mirroring process described so far excludes women and subjects who do not conform to the hetero-patriarchal norm. Albinati cannot give an account of the experiences of women and victims with which he does not identify precisely because of his gender positioning and because of the testimonial ethos that characterizes, notwithstanding its ambiguities, the autofiction genre. This practice, which coherently aligns with the method of the *partire da sé* as well as with the aforementioned attempt to deconstruct sexist discourse, problematically deprives a great part of the novel of a perspective that cannot but be crucial in feminist representations of gender violence and femicide. Moreover, *La scuola cattolica* runs the risk of consolidating the process of male-based universalization through the vicious repetition of an androcentric literary discourse (and canon) that does not allow space for the expression of female gender difference (Schweickart 1986:42).

In light of this, the obliteration of women's voice in Albinati's book seems to corroborate Stanley's theories on auto/biography, according to which male gender positioning inhibits the production of feminist narratives because feminism is an ontological condition that can only be grasped by subjects who experimented patriarchal oppression (1995:253). The problem with Stanley's argument is the harshly dichotomous approach with which she interprets the relationship between men and women as well as that between the victimizer and the victimized. Albinati challenges this distinction at the end of the novel, where the autofiction blurs into a narration based on entirely unverifiable events (the supposed statutory rape) and where the frequency of omissions guarantees a fruitful generalized identification of the readers. Here, the de-structuration of male authoriality allows the narrator to recognize his own positioning as oppressor (in light of his adherence to the patriarchal system of values) and, at the same time, as oppressed (as someone who was presumably abused during childhood). This polysemy, or impossibility to label the subject according to a rigidly binary classification, does not correspond to the negation of the historical oppression of the masculine on the feminine, which is widely documented in the text. On the contrary, it contributes to the process of sabotaging the symbolic apparatus by questioning the distinction between active males and passive females that legitimizes gender discriminations (Bourdieu 2002:7–8). This feminist discursive operation is furtherly sustained by the act, which is also undertaken by the narrator in the last part of the book, of addressing female characters as interlocutors and subjects.

By virtue of a renewed contact with the category of the feminine, male authorship progressively loses its conformity to the hegemonic model and becomes Other, thus overcoming the limitations imposed by gender polarization. In this regard, the suspension of coherence in the representation of the self that the receiver witnesses while reading *La scuola cattolica* can be interpreted as a fruitful practice aimed at troubling the cultural violence that strongly invites the subject to align to the socially constructed gender prototypes (Butler 2005:42) from which violence arises.

Notes

1 Albinati is a writer, translator and teacher in the Rebibbia penitentiary. His literary works include *Maggio selvaggio* (1999), *Il ritorno. Diario di una missione in Afghanistan* (2002), and *Vita e morte di un ingegnere* (2012). After *La scuola cattolica*, Albinati published *Un adulterio* (2017). On Albinati's work, see Ricciardi (2011) and Bonfili (2016).

2 Among other things, 2016 was the year of the killing of Sara Di Pietrantonio, a 22-year-old woman strangled and set on fire in Rome by her ex-partner, Vincenzo Paduano. The crime's brutality generated substantial media attention and caused feminist demonstrations that resulted in the formation of the network of feminist groups and collectives Non una di meno. On Sara Di Pietrantionio's case and its journalistic coverage see Mandolini (2020).

3 This model is suggested, among other things, by the tendencies that characterize the reading of journalistic articles since the beginning of the new millennium, when reading moved from the hard-copy to the online, which is governed by the principles of multiplicity (of sources and perspectives) and agility. On this, see Gazoia (2016:114–116).

4 The first consciousness raising group was created in New York in 1967, by the activists of the New York Radical Women. On this, see Brownmiller 1999: "The Founders." In Italy, the practice was imported by Carla Lonzi, a guiding figure of Italian feminism and founder of the Roman collective Rivolta femminile, who established the first *autocoscienza* group, thus promoting the dissemination of consciousness raising in the rest of the peninsula during the first years of the 1970s. On *autocoscienza*, see Libreria delle donne di Milano (1987:32–35) and Lonzi (2010:115–120).

5 In addition to the mentions of Izzo's second femicide committed in 2005, a demonstration of Albinati's interest in interpreting the crimes of the Circeo massacre as precursors of gendered abuses carried out in contemporary times is a passage where the narrator makes reference to another case of lethal sexist violence – the murder of fourteen years old at the hands of a group of teenagers, which occurred in Leno in 2002. After recalling the vicious case, the protagonist explains that the book's objective is to describe

a "long struggle of liberation [that of women against patriarchal oppression] that is far from being over." (Albinati 2019:VII.4)

6 Connell hypothesized the existence of a hierarchical system within which different typologies of masculinity co-exist. According to the theorist, the top position is occupied by hegemonic masculinity, a category that flexibly adapts to historical and geographical contexts, though it rigidly imposes dogmas on gendered behaviors. Notwithstanding the practical impossibility of conforming to hegemonic masculinity, the category offers a model of dominant virility that guarantees the perpetuation of patriarchal culture (2005:76–77). This concept is perfectly expressed by Albinati in the following sentence: "Since the majority of males do not correspond to the image of the male, [...] this demonstrates that to be a male means to be not as somebody actually is, but as somebody should be." (2019:II.4)

7 Sociological studies have demonstrated how sexual liaisons with women and hyperbolic talks about them have the function to guarantee the impression of an adherence to the model of hegemonic masculinity in the context of homosocial relationships (Flood 2008:341–341; Ferrero Camoletto 2013:67–68).

8 This association is confirmed by the narrator's reference to the "use of 'recovered memories,'" which is described as a psychotherapy technique aimed "at bringing to surface memories buried in the subconscious, especially concerning sex abuse suffered in childhood." (X.12) However, this mention does not resolve the text's ambiguity, as the narrator asks himself: "Authentic abuse, or the product of outside suggestion? That is, created by the very same therapy that should do nothing more than recover them?" (X.12) On trauma recollections as a non-linear and fragmented narrative practice, see Herman (1997:37) and Brison (1999:41).

Works cited

Albinati, E. (1999) *Maggio selvaggio*. Milan: Mondadori.

Albinati, E. (2002) *Il ritorno. Diario di una missione in Afghanistan*. Milan: Mondadori.

Albinati, E. (2012) *Vita e morte di un ingegnere*. Milan: Mondadori.

Albinati, E. (2016a) *La scuola cattolica*. Milan: Rizzoli.

Albinati, E. (2016b) "L'esigenza di tenerezza del maschio," in Rangeri, N., Di Genova, A. and Pagliaru, A. Il corpo del delitto. *Il Manifesto*. November 9. pp. 51–52.

Albinati, E. (2017) *Un adulterio*. Milan: Rizzoli.

Albinati, E. (2019) [e-book] *The Catholic School*. Transl. A. Shuugar. London: Picador.

Anderson, K. L. and Umberson, D. (2001) "Gendering Violence: Masculinity and Power in Men's Account of Domestic Violence," *Gender & Society* 15(3):358–380.

Bonfili, S. (2016) "Edoardo Albinati: Irrealtà o inganno della realtà?" *Heteroglossia* 14:273–290.

Booth, W. C. (1983) *The Rhetoric of Fiction*. Chicago and London: University of Chicago Press.

Brison, S. (1999) "Trauma Narratives and the Remaking of the Self," in Bale, M., Crewe, V. J. and Spitzer, L. (eds.), *Acts of Memory: Cultural Recall in the Present*. Hanover and London: University Press of New England, pp. 34–54.

Bourdieu, P. (2002) [1998] *Masculine Domination*. Transl. R. Nice. Bloomington: Stanford University Press.

Butler, J. (2005) *Giving an Account of Oneself*. New York: Fordham University Press.

Cigarini, L. (1995) *La politica del desiderio*. Muraro, L., and Rampello, L. (eds.). Parma: Nuova Pratiche Editrice.

Connell, R. (2005) [1995] *Masculinities*. Berkeley and Los Angeles: University of California Press.

Cortellessa, A. (2016) *La scuola cattolica* cova il delitto del Circeo. *LaStampa*. March 19: https://www.lastampa.it/tuttolibri/2016/03/19/news/la-scuola-cattolica-cova-il-delitto-del-circeo-1.37627052. Accessed 9 December 2020.

Doubrovsky, S. (1977) *Fils*. Paris: Galilée.

Eco, U. (1979) *Lector in fabula. La cooperazione interpretativa nei testi narrativi*. Milan: Bompiani.

Farrell, W. T. (1972) "Male Consciousness-Raising from a Sociological and Political Perspective," *Sociological Focus* 5(2):19–28.

Ferrero Camoletto, R. (2013) "Ridere e parlare di sesso: una costruzione plurale delle maschilità eterosessuali," *Salute e società* 3:59–76.

Flood, M. (2008) "Men, Sex, and Homosociality. How Bonds between Men Shape Their Sexual Relations with Women," *Men and Masculinities* 10(3):339–359.

FRA. (2014) *Violence Against Women: An EU-Wide-Survey*. Luxemburg: Publication Office of the European Union.

Gasperina Geroni, R. (2018a) "Il *thinking slow* e l'arte del ragionare. Una conversazione con Edoardo Albinati," *The Italianist* 38(1):126–133.

Gasperina Geroni, R. (2018b) "Gli anni Settanta tra violenza di genere e decostruzione del maschile: *La scuola cattolica* di Edoardo Albinati," *The Italianist* 38(1):108–125.

Gazoia, A. (2016) *Senza filtro. Chi controlla l'informazione*. Rome: Minimum Fax.

Goldner, V., Penn, P. S. and Walker, M. E. G. (1990) "Violence and Love. Gender Paradoxes in Volatile Attachments," *Family Process* 29:343–364.

Herman, J. (1997) *Trauma and Recovery. The Aftermath of Violence – From Domestic Abuse to Political Terror*. New York: Basic Books.

Libreria delle donne di Milano. (1987) *Non credere di avere dei diritti*. Turin: Rosenberg & Seller.

Lonzi, C. (2010) [1974] *Sputiamo su Hegel*. Milan: Et al.

Mandolini, N. (2020) "Femminicidio, prima e dopo. Un'analisi qualitativa della copertura giornalistica dei casi Stefania Noce (2011) e Sara Di Pietrantonio (2016)," *Problemi dell'informazione* 65(2):246–277.

Marchese, L. (2014) *L'io possibile, l'autofiction come paradosso del romanzo contemporaneo*. Massa: Transeuropa.

Raimo, C. (2016) *La scuola cattolica* di Albinati svela la violenza dei maschi italiani. *Internazionale*. April 10: https://www.internazionale.it/opinione/christian-raimo/2016/04/10/scuola-cattolica-albinati-recensione. Accessed 15 December 2020.

Ricciardi, S. (2011) *Gli artifici della non-fiction: la messinscena narrativa in Albinati, Franchini e Veronesi*. Massa: Transeuropa.

Savettieri, C. (2018) "Il saggismo ambiguo della *Scuola cattolica*." *Allegoria* 76:125–136.

Schweickart, P. P. (1986) "Reading Ourselves: Toward a Feminist Theory of Reading," in Flynn, E. and Schweickart, P. P. (eds.), *Gender and Reading. Essays on Readers, Texts, and Contexts*. Baltimore: Johns Hopkins University Press, pp. 31–62.

Stanley, L. (1995) *The Auto/biographical I: The Theory and Practice of Feminist Auto/Biography*. Manchester: Manchester University Press.

8 Rewriting the myth: *Padreterno* (2015) by Caterina Serra

Published in 2015 by the major Italian publishing house Einaudi and already object of critical discussions (Bazzoni 2020), *Padreterno* by Caterina Serra[1] addresses lethal gender violence by means of a re-narration and actualization of a tale borrowed from Greek mythology, that of the demi-god Aristaeus. The myth of Aristaeus, which was recounted in epic poems such as Hesiod's *Theogony* and Virgil's *Georgics*, tells the story of Apollo and Cyrene's son, who was born in Libya following the rape of the nymph by the god. After growing up with the centaur Chiron and the Muses, Aristaeus marries Autonoe, but he falls in love with Orpheus' wife, the nymph Eurydice, who dies poisoned by a snake while she is trying to escape the demi-god who wants to rape her. Eurydice's death foments the anger of the nymphs, who punish the beekeeper Aristaeus provoking the die-off of his bees. It is only through the help of his mother, a raped nymph herself, that the demi-god decides to sacrifice eight head of cattle from whose bellies the bees will resurrect.

In *Padreterno*, Aristaeus' myth serves as the allegorical substratum that sustains the characters' and plot's construction. The intertextual reference to the mythological story is made explicit by the use of the name Aristeo (the Italian version of "Aristaeus") to refer to the protagonist, as well as by his declared passion for bee-keeping. Moreover, the link to the classical tale is repeatedly spelled out, together with other mentions of the Greek and Roman mythological tradition in the novel itself, which testifies to Serra's choice to carry out a straightforward renarration that openly dialogs with the original story in order to produce a metatextual interweaving.

As opposed to the texts analyzed so far, *Padreterno* explores the narrative dimension of the purely fictional. This is because myths that lose their original connection to the principle of faith and are no longer considered credible are comparable to fictional texts for the effect they

DOI: 10.4324/9781003120339-8

have in the recipient's imaginary (Frye 1961:599–600). However, if compared to literature, myth is characterized by a higher degree of trustworthiness because it is commonly employed in scientific, philosophical, and artistic discourses (599). This is exemplified, among other things, by Sigmund Freud's extensive use of mythology to validate his psychoanalytic theories. The widespread adoption of myths in the realm of discourses criticized for disseminating a male-centered rhetoric (Freud's theories, for example) is precisely what determined feminist interpretation of mythology as a patriarchal set of narratives that need to be de-structured and adapted to women's representative needs (Pollock 2006:103–104). Along with the practice of deconstructing sexist myths, writers and theorists have contributed to the resymbolization and rehabilitation of minor mythical tales that could be used for (re)creating feminist genealogies and tropes (103). Serra chooses this second path and recuperates an unexplored episode of classical mythology in order to give it new space within the realm of feminist cultural memory. *Padreterno* assigns to Aristaeus' myth, which had been obscured by the adjacent myth of Orpheus, a prominence that contributes to its re-signification as an allegory of hegemonic masculinity in crisis.

The text's structure and plot are testimony to Serra's interest in using the myth to deconstruct the idea of firmness that is often linked to virility and (toxic) masculinity. The book consists of a long monologue divided into forty brief chapters. Here, the protagonist, Aristeo, tells his dying father the series of actions that led to the femicide of his partner, Nina, and to the consequent blight on his bees. Following the mythical path, Nina corresponds to Eurydice, after whose death, the killer needs to sacrifice something to win his bees back. Serra's Aristeo will decide to symbolically sacrifice his father by bringing him home just before his death, thus facilitating the return of the bees.

This synopsis illustrates *Padreterno*'s effort to represent the relationship between father and son by means of a metanarrative strategy. It is through the intertwining of Aristeo's narrative with that of his father that the problematic process of mirroring with and rejection of the fatherly figure is presented to the reader. The protagonist's father is portrayed as a storyteller whose interest in mythology frequently brought him to narrate Greek and Roman mythical tales to his son:

> Do you remember when you used to tell me the story of Zeus who slips between Danae's legs as a golden shower? You used to say

> that in that way he possessed her, as if to possess was gentler than to screw. When I told that to Nina, she said that maybe you meant to say to rape. (Serra 2015:4)

As this passage demonstrates, the father's storytelling practice contributes to the circulation of the patriarchal rhetoric that underestimates and normalizes acts of violence against women. This is opposed by Nina's feminist counter-discourse and, to some extent, by Aristeo's own progressive separation from his father's speech. As the novel advances, it becomes clear how the father's alignment to a patriarchal system of values based on the idea of male possession, which is conveyed by his implicit association to the figure of the storyteller Orpheus[2] and by his sympathy for major mythical events, is challenged by Aristeo's practice of resymbolization of a minor tale that clashes with misogynist logic.[3] The metanarrative structure imposed by the presence of the storytelling theme activates a *mise en abîme* of the rewriting operation undertaken by Serra: just as Aristeo challenges his father's patriarchal discourse reassigning centrality to a peripheral myth, the author rereads a mythical story of femicide through a feminist lens.

The title, *Padreterno* [Heavenly Father], also suggests the novel's thematic focus on the topic of fatherhood, here intended as a semantic area where the issues of male genealogy and authority intersect. In the text, the word *padreterno* only appears once in the context of a reflection authored by Nina and reported by Aristeo to his father:

> Nina says that the fault is of intrusive and petulant mothers, those who want to control, those who obsess over the malechild, all one word, as she pronounces it. Those who fill him with attentions and encouragements, with glorifications and reprimands. [...] That malechild who, in the end, will feel like that for the rest of his life. A heavenlyfather, all one word, as she pronounces it. I don't know, Dad. Maybe it's because she doesn't have children. She always regrets saying that. That it's the mothers' fault. (Serra 2015:141–142)

Here, Nina underscores the genealogical dimension by associating the expression "heavenlyfather" [*padreterno*] to "malechild" [*figliomaschio*]. The link is suggested by the fact that both expressions are lexical units and identify specific phases in the construction of male gendered identity: the phase of adoration experienced during childhood (*figliomaschio*/"malechild") as well as the consequent attitude toward domination and arrogance that characterizes adulthood (*padreterno*/"heavenly father"). In light of this, the expression *padreterno* can be referred both to the character of Aristeo – the son of an idolizing mother who, before the final conversion, will kill Nina as a result of his despotic mindset – and to the protagonist's father. Notwithstanding the implicit reference to the theme of male genealogy, this passage blames mothers for raising their male children as subjects who will subsequently conform to the patriarchal paradigm of the *padreterno*. This idea, which seems antithetical to Nina's feminist positioning, coherently matches Serra's decision to avoid any simplistic and ideological exculpation of female figures who, despite their unequivocal position as victims of sexist violence, promote affective and educative models that contribute to preserve the patriarchal social order.

To better understand the relational dynamics that connect *Padreterno*'s characters, it is necessary to analyze the way they employ Aristeo's mythical name and their use of alternative epithets. For example, Aristeo's mother, Barbara, calls his son "Teo," which emphasizes the part of the name that "means god," (16) as the narrating voice explicitly refers to the reader. This nominative practice is coherently matched by the woman's propensity to educate her son according to the model of hegemonic masculinity and to the idea of male (omni) potence. Barbara's confidence in Aristeo's ability to get whatever he wants (53) is confirmed by her venerational behaviors: she is recalled by the protagonist while she kneels at her kid's feet (15) and while she reverently cooks his favorite fritters (56).

However, the hierarchy that characterizes the relationship between mother and son is not linear. Barbara's attitude toward Aristeo is ambiguous: on the one hand, she idolizes him as a god, thus putting herself in the subaltern position that women should occupy according to patriarchal precepts; on the other side, her conduct reveals a tendency toward possession and power that her role of parent allows. This double connotation of the mother as a loving and, at the same time, dominating subject is well exemplified by this passage:

> Why should we teach ourselves how to be better than what we are? If we feel strong, if we always meet a woman who likes us this way? It's the mother [...] She used to cut my nails once per week, on Saturdays. I was standing and she sat on the toilet seat. The nails fell on her lap, between her knees. Each nail she cut she moved her lips and kissed the top of my toe. When she was done, she grabbed the hem of her skirt and threw my ten nails into the

> toilet. My nails, together with my non-requested declaration of independence. (60)

The adult Aristeo describes his mother as a woman who condones arrogance by carrying out caring and submissive actions. Notwithstanding this, the act of cutting the son's nails has a double and ambiguous value: it denotes cure and devotion but it also can be interpreted in terms of an appropriation of the other's body, as testified by Aristeo's own statement about the loss of his autonomy.

This portrayal aligns with feminist theories that describe motherly position in patriarchal societies as a condition of power and lack of power at the same time (Nicholson 1993; Rich 1972; Ruddick 1995). The Italian theorist Lea Melandri draws on these insights to describe the mother as "the body that held [the male child] in thrall when he was completely dependent and defenceless, the body that could give him life or death, nurturing or abandonment." (2011:98) In other words, mothers in patriarchy play the role of submitted submitters toward their male children, thus contributing to the reproduction of what Melandri calls "the armed powerlessness of the man-child." (96) Patriarchal tendency to symbolically collapse the category of womanhood into that of motherhood then determines the reproduction of the relational model that men experienced during childhood in their adult emotional ties with women. Intimate partner violence against women is the result of that concoction of insecurity and desire for domination that the man-child perceives following the abandonment of a female partner who he sees as he saw his mother (97–98). In this sense, Serra portrays Barbara as the unaware generator of that relational dependency that Aristeo will replicate in his sentimental liaisons and that will bring him to kill Nina.

In *Padreterno*, mothers' participation in the psycho-social dynamics that lead to femicide is never represented as the result of women's free decision, and, for this reason, it cannot be interpreted as simplistic mother blaming. On the contrary, it serves as a tool to portray the intricate mechanisms that regulate the vicious circle of the sexist yoke. Aristeo's mother, for example, is introduced to the readers as a "boring, bustling, and obsessive housewife" who adapted to her husband's controlling attitude (Serra 2015:9) and had no choice but to submit to his psychological (21) and physical violence (97–98). The father, vice-versa, is depicted as the holder of a privilege that assigns him power and, consequently, blame. His name, Giovanni, contains an etymological reference to the act of naming and knowing (150), which further reinforces the idea of his agency. He is presented as the figure who divulges patriarchal dogmas through storytelling and he is the only character who respects the mythological mention, thus referring to Aristeo using his full name. His patriarchal possessive attitude is confirmed by the tendency to exercise direct violence on his wife when he perceives that his authority is endangered. The protagonist recalls one of his father's abusive reactions, which is triggered by the sight of Barbara and Aristeo's loving complicity. Giovanni rapes his wife and rants against mother and son saying: "You are alike, you are against me, I see you always together, you talk quietly, you hide in the toilet." (97–98) Here, the need to reestablish his dominion on his wife's body corresponds to the phenomenon of menaced virility described by Melandri; in other words, it is the consequence of the fear of being deprived of the woman's attention. Aristeo insists on this aspect by recognizing the signs of a male genealogy marked by possessiveness in his father's behavior. He states: "You were jealous. Weren't you? You too, a lonely child, at the center of the life of a mother who was like mine." (135) The mother's complicity in the maintenance of patriarchal culture is reiterated in this passage, but subjects who identify with the male gender are those who are clearly assigned the responsibility of preserving the existing socio-symbolic order. It is not a coincidence that the violent actions carried out by the protagonist are modeled on those of his father and that only Giovanni's death will permit Aristeo to break the patriarchal vicious circle.

The father exerts a significant influence on the son's imaginary and it is on the symbolic associations that he introduces that the novel's allegoric apparatus is shaped. For example, he is the first to suggest the correlation between bees and women that legitimizes Aristeo's gender violence:

> You invented a story about the revenge of bees, killer bees you called them, with their queen who smelled the odor of the kid who had disturbed them. Do you remember? The queen who chased me [...] Mom used to tell us to stop, otherwise, I would have been left scared of bees and females. (76)

The demonization of the bees-women is made possible by the father's narrative, which serves as a behavioral model that confirms the self-representation as a victim that the violent man proposes as a result of a constant actualization of the relationship with the mother. The metaphor of the bees suggests that Aristeo's violent behavior toward woman is deeply intertwined with his own fear of them. The recognition of the female Other as dangerous is, in fact, what triggers the abusive reactions, as demonstrated by the protagonist's beating and killing of his partner, which is portrayed as a clear result of Aristeo's fear of being hurt and abandoned.

The rhetorical overturning of the patriarchal fatherly narrative is carried out, in *Padreterno*, by the character of Nina, the woman who, despite ending up victimized by Aristeo, guides him toward the destitution of the paradigm of hegemonic masculinity. This is anticipated by her frequent use of the epithet "Aris," which deprives the name Aristeo of its godlike hint and refers etymologically to the idea of integrity and nobility. The prominent function exercised by Nina's discourse is proved by the presence at the beginning of each chapter, of brief poems written on receipts that the woman left for Aristeo in the domestic space they shared. The poem-receipts represent the victim's authoriality and they oppose patriarchal justifying rhetoric by offering a fair portrayal of the roles of victims and perpetrators:

> *Hi, mon*
> *petit chien.*
> *I slept*
> *on the floor.*
> *Maybe*
> *your dog*
> *am I.*
> *You pretend*
> *not*
> *to know*
> *how to do.*
> *And you take*
> *everything.*
> *With your ego*
> *that wags its tail*
> *and doesn't let me*
> *stand.* (20)

With the metaphor of the dog, which is generally employed to denote a subordinate position, Nina gives an account of her partner's tendency to instrumentally use his supposed psychological weakness to victimize and relegate her to an actual position of inferiority. In her poems, the woman expresses the objectification into which Aristeo forces her but she also uses them as a communicative space where to affirm her own individuality and to refer to her desire for change. In so doing, Nina offers the positive image of an agentic and communicative female subject, thus freeing herself from the stereotype of the passive victim.

The woman also resymbolizes the bees by recognizing them as an emblem of desirable female independence and power, which is precisely the same quality that characterizes them as abject and frightening creatures. In one of her poetic notes, Nina labels the bees as a model for self-determination against male domestication. This is how the note reads in the context of the protagonist's monologue:

> *I would like to be*
> *one of your*
> *bees.*
> *I should*
> *learn*
> *from them*
> *how to*
> *live without*
> *a man.* (39)

In another poetic note that precedes the reference to the story of the killer bees, Nina portrays herself as a bee who stings Aristeo (73), thus activating an identification process that testifies to her desire for emancipation from the violent liaison. With the continuation of the novel, Nina's rhetorical operation contributes to changing Aristeo's perception of his own dysfunctional relationality, which ultimately results in the man's decision to sacrifice the symbol of patriarchal power, his father, to the bees.

At first, the man's relationship with Nina's feminist counter-discourse is conflictual and the poems are often followed by Aristeo's negative statements on his partner. Similarly, the protagonist frequently expresses his will of silencing the woman (18;35;68;69;137), which will be enforced with the femicide (186). However, after Nina's disappearance, this desire is substituted with a feeling of loss that coincides with the nostalgia for the woman's voice, as demonstrated by the murderer's words: "Do not leave me like that. Speak, please, say something. Talk to me, Nina, talk to me." (187) The consequences of the lethal deed (Nina's absence and silence) generate an awareness in the man and a sense of responsibility that Aristeo never manifested after the previous violent acts, as confirmed by what he says in the monologue to his father: "I did not want to hurt her, as the other times. But I did it. This is what I wanted to tell you. I did not even realize it. It is that last time that I understood. That I killed her, Dad." (187–188) Notwithstanding the presence of phrases that deny the perpetrator's intentionality, Aristeo's discourse is not self-absolving and concludes with a clear declaration of guilt. Nina's femicide, which in the passage is explicitly portrayed as the result of a long series of abuses, is also presented as the event that activates the storytelling process ("This is what I wanted to tell you"). In this sense, the whole retelling of Aristeo's story can be interpreted as the abusive man's attempt to atone for the femicide by means of a new encounter with Nina that happens on the narrative plane.

We can analyze Aristeo's new and "textual" relationship with the woman by making reference to the theories developed by Jessica Benjamin. In *Beyond Doer and Done To* (2018), a volume on abusive relationality and the strategies adopted to overcome it, Benjamin states that the abuser's tendency to put the blame on the Other (which is demonstrated by Aristeo in the first part of the novel) characterizes dyadic and complementary relationships where a lack of mutual recognition determines the irrational perception of the partner as disrespectful, which in turn results in violence (2018:24–25). It is only by realizing the effect that his actions have on the Other's subjectivity that the possibility of opening a space of communication where differences do not collapse but meet materializes. This space, called "thirdness," is described by Benjamin as the dimension where the radical separation between subject and object from which violence stems is surmounted and the subject frees himself "from any intent to control or coerce." (24) Following Nina's departure, the space of thirdness can only be that of narration, which is the virtual territory where the narrator dialogs with his partner. The fact that the woman's poems punctuate the man's monologue testifies to this dialogic effort and delineates a progression in the quality of the interaction. In fact, it is precisely by gradually taking into account Nina's authorial voice that Aristeo decides to abandon the previously endorsed model of toxic masculinity.

In the wake of his admission of responsibility, the protagonist reevaluates Nina's compositions recognizing them as "an expression of trust," as "one of those actions carried out in silence, in the shade, with gratitude. As the bees make honey." (Serra 2015:193) By finally assigning a positive connotation to the woman-bee simile, the narrator welcomes Nina's words and lets himself go to a polyphonic narration that combines his new desire to emancipate from the rigidity of gender compartimentalization and the female subject's voicing. When, after the symbolic sacrifice of his father (the patriarchal model), the bees reoccupy Aristeo's house transforming it in a big hive, the narrator dismisses his controlling attitude and opens himself up to a mutual recognition with them: "They recognize me now. I learned, I am not scared anymore, I love them, I set them free, I get what they give to me." (189) The change of behavior toward the bees corresponds to Aristeo's rebirth as well as to his acceptance of the dimension of thirdness conceptualized by Benjamin and evoked in the novel's concluding remarks, which showcase the protagonist's interest in exploring alternative forms of identity that do not conform to the gender polarization offered by patriarchal structures:

> I don't know. I will invent something. Maybe I will become that third thing that you can become. That third thing that is not the result of birth or choice. That third thing that does not relate to the guilt of one's father or the will of one's mother. (194)

The open ending proposed by Serra, in this sense, functions as a narrative device that supports the reconceptualization of the perpetrator's subjectivity beyond the principle of dominant masculinity and challenges the patriarchal gender binarism that keeps legitimizing the split between abusive males and victimized females. This indeterminacy, which permits *Padreterno* to be labeled as an open work (Eco 1989) and proves crucial to the process of identification, impels the reader to imagine types of subjectivities that overcome the dogma of gender binarism.

Padreterno's mythical re-narration examines lethal gender violence by interrogating the psychosocial construction of masculinity. As already seen in the case of *La scuola cattolica*, Serra's work aligns with feminist ethos despite adopting a narratological perspective focussed on the perpetrator. However, the novel includes a female and victim-centered perspective (Nina's poems) that Albinati could not consider because of his positioning as a male narrator in the context of an autofictional text. This operation is guaranteed by Serra's decision to engage with a narrative typology that is fully independent of references to the writer's gender position and to specific real events. Despite the presence of some limitations imposed by the mythical intertext, *Padreterno*'s purely fictional dimension facilitates the employment of a double first-person narrative that integrates male and female perspectives and ultimately supports the overcoming of rigid gender distinctions. Moreover, metatextuality and symbolism – both characteristics that distinguish open literary works, as testified by the last part of Albinati's book – make it possible to incorporate the female character's discourse into that of the male narrator creating the effect of an intersubjective exchange rather than that of a patriarchal appropriation.

The presence of the double narratological point of view also guarantees the possibility of mirroring for subjects who identify with the male and female gender alike. In addition, the frequent use of the open form of poetry and Serra's evocative rather than descriptive narrative style support the activation of an identification process that allows receivers to take part in the creation of meaning regardless of their gender positioning. This couples with an unsettling representation of masculinity (usually portrayed as weak, though violent) and femininity (usually portrayed as agentive, though victimized) that contributes to subverting the readers' expectations and asks them to participate in the practice of gender resymbolization. It is precisely in this regard that *Padreterno* proves successful, given its ability to describe the complexities that determine the gender hierarchies from which sexist violence originates without renouncing the effort of rhetorically overcoming them by means of an intersubjective narrative practice that defeats the process of domination.

Notes

1 Before *Padreterno*, Serra published the novel *Tilt* (2008), an adaptation from the reportage *Chiusa in una stanza sempre aperta*, which the author wrote in 2006. Serra also works as screenwriter and editor.

2 The myth of Orpheus has been interpreted as a patriarchal tale in which the female figure of Eurydice is instrumentally immolated for the sake of the man's possession and desire to be glorified as a poet. As feminist scholarship noted, Orpheus' decision to turn and transgress Hades' rule by watching Eurydice and condemn her to remain in the underworld provides the storyteller with lifeblood for his poetic compositions (Locke 2000:2).

3 If, in the case of Orpheus, the sexist annihilation of the female figure is not direct and the bard never admits, regrets and pays back for his possessive attitude, in the case of Aristaeus, the act of causing Eurydice's death is followed by a reparative gesture that implies an admission of responsibility.

Works cited

Bazzoni, A. (2020) Una voce violenta. Intervista a Caterina Serra, autrice di *Padreterno* (Einaudi 2015). *Nuovi argomenti*. January 20: http://www.nuoviargomenti.net/una-voce-violenta-intervista-a-caterina-serra-autrice-di-padreterno-einaudi-2015/. Accessed 22 January 2021.

Benjamin, J. (2018) *Beyond Doer and Done To. Recognition Theory, Intersubjectivity, and the Third.* London and New York: Routledge.

Eco, U. (1989) [1962] *The Open Work*. Transl. A. Concogni. Cambridge, Massachusetts: Harvard University Press.

Frye, N. (1961) "Myth, Fiction, and Displacement," *Dedalus* 90.3:587–605.

Locke, L. (2000) *Eurydice's Body: Feminist Reflection on the Orphic Descent Myth in Philosophy and Film*. Indiana University. PhD Thesis.

Melandri, L. (2011) *Amore e violenza: il fattore molesto della civiltà*. Turin: Bollato Boringhieri.

Nicholson, P. (1993) "Motherhood and Women's Lives," in Robinson, V. and Richardson, D. (eds.), *Introducing Women's Studies. Feminist Theory and Practice*. London: Palgrave, pp. 201–233.

Pollock, G. (2006) "Beyond Oedipus: Feminist Thought, Psychoanalysis, and Mythical Figurations of the Feminine," in Zajko, V. and Leonard, M. (eds.), *Laughing with Medusa. Classical Myth and Feminist Thought*. Oxford: Oxford University Press, pp. 67–117.

Rich, A. (1972) "When We Dead Awaken: Writing as Re-Vision," *College English* 34(1):18–30.

Ruddick, S. (1995) *Maternal Thinking. Towards a Politics of Peace*. Boston: Beacon Press.

Serra, C. (2008) *Tilt*. Turin: Einaudi.

Serra, C. (2015) *Padreterno*. Turin: Einaudi.

Conclusions

Femicide in Italy is a vicious prevalent crime whose connections to the area of cultural and symbolic gender discrimination deserve continuous scholarly scrutiny. It is only through this work of documentation, analysis, and denunciation, as well as through a constant dialog between academic circles and the areas of political intervention and activism, that efficacious practices can be implemented with the aim of directly counteracting the phenomenon.

In the Italian context, feminist activists and scholars have proved successful in bringing to the fore the issue of lethal gender-based victimization. The mainstreaming of the feminist discourse on femicide has already produced significant achievements both in the sphere of legislation and in that of public awareness. Italy now has a law that protects victims of stalking (legge n. 38, 2009), and femicide – a widely known phenomenon among Italian citizens of all ages – is officially recognized as a crime in the country. However, the rate of femicide is far from declining on the Italian peninsula. The number of gender-based murders of women in 2020 remained stable, while a dramatic increase (+73%) of emergency calls received by the institutional line established by the local Minister for gender equality was registered between March and April 2020 (Rossitto 2020) because of the COVID-19 pandemic and the related lockdown. Activists have repeatedly blamed institutions for their negligence in recognizing the areas of prevention and education as specific sites for the implementation of measures aimed at tackling patriarchal social structures and culture that allow femicide to occur. In particular, a lack of government funding directed at women's shelters and feminist organizations that promote educational projects on the phenomenon has been denounced in recent years (Biaggioni and Pirrone 2018:17–18; D.i.Re 2019; Camilli 2020).

Moreover, numerous controversies still dominate the area of communication and narrative production on the topic, as the development

DOI: 10.4324/9781003120339-102

of a metadiscourse on the portrayal of lethal gender violence demonstrates. In the specific sphere of representation, Italian feminist scholars and activists' concerns about the outcomes of the mainstreaming of feminist debates on femicide abound. The widespread employment of the concept of *femminicidio* in Italian journalistic coverages of murder cases and media discussions has been associated with a tendency to adopt compensatory rhetorical strategies that reproduce gender stereotypes and fail to discursively contrast the deep symbolic gender imbalance that legitimizes sexist abuse (Abis and Orrù 2016; Giomi 2015, 2019; Mandolini 2020). In other words, patriarchal discourse superficially adapts itself in order not to succumb to the emergence of a counter-discourse (the feminist one on femicide, in our case) that challenges it; as a result, it absorbs some of the rhetorical features of the counter-discourse and expropriates the latter of its subversive traits. It is precisely for this reason that an analysis of narratives that engage with the issue of lethal gender violence is crucial to unveil the practices that contribute to change or conversely, to maintain the *status quo*.

This volume adds to existing scholarly research in the field by proposing a study of the contribution that journalistic inquiries and literary works make to the popularization of feminist discourse on femicide in the Italian context.

The analysis of the representation of femicide in journalistic inquiries suggests the presence of a general tendency to criticize the simplified depiction of the phenomenon offered by newspaper coverage. Following the counter-informative approach that pertains to the genre of Italian investigative journalism, reporters propose narrations that are influenced by the feminist metadiscourse on the portrayal of lethal gender violence, albeit at different levels. These narrations generally call for a respectful, non-spectacularized and non-stereotypical representation of the victim and events as well as for an actual stigmatization of the perpetrator. However, this does not necessarily guarantee the text's ability to conform to a feminist ethos. This is the case with Fiorucci's work, where the counter-informative approach proves to be only a cosmetic stance that is not backed by an actual effort to overcome patriarchal clichés on gender abuse. In other instances, such as those of Iacona and Maiorana, the alignment to feminist metadiscourse is much more accurate. Notwithstanding the persistence of problematic aspects borrowed from the same metadiscourse (for example, Iacona's heterosexism and Maiorana's rigidly victim-centered approach), here the mainstreaming of feminist reflections fosters a commendable depiction of the specific events narrated and of femicide as a national social issue.

The reading also shows the decisive role played in the representation by stylistic features and, in particular, by the intertwinement of journalistic and literary narrative devices (what Buonanno labeled as *faction*). For example, the presence of the traditionally literary practice of fictionalization in the works of Fiorucci and Maiorana was linked to the production of a stereotypical portrayal that, despite triggering indignation through emphasis, did not always respect the complexity of the reality it referred to. Conversely, the adoption of an (inter)subjective narration, as observed in Iacona's and Maiorana's inquiries, was demonstrated to successfully contrast the reduction of figures and actions to crystallized clichés by maintaining a partial but direct contact with the events and, at the same time, by stimulating the readers' mirroring with characters and situations mentioned in the text.

Literary works, on the other hand, present explicit or implicit references to the feminist debate on femicide. Furthermore, the emergence of the debate is unequivocally linked to an increase in the production of literature that examines lethal gender violence, notwithstanding the presence of an earlier Italian literary tradition on the more general topic of patriarchal abuse. The analysis conducted on the selected texts does not allow to identify common tendencies in the way femicide is represented. Some works (a few stories included in *Nessuna più*, *La scuola cattolica* and *Padreterno*) successfully deconstruct stereotypes commonly associated with victims and perpetrators of gender violence, thus contributing to overcoming the symbolic order that naturalizes the opposition between femininity and masculinity. Other texts (*Fiore… come me* and the remaining stories included in *Nessuna più*) maintain gender clichés and, despite superficially denouncing femicide, they remain anchored to the rigidity of patriarchal dichotomies.

This present study confirms the already noticed propensity of open narratives to guarantee a more respectful and inclusive representation of gendered violence (Cucklanz 2000:154–160; Giomi and Magaraggia 2017:56; Moorti 2002:116). Open narratives have different characteristics (e.g. subjective narration, presence of textual omissions, lack of a proper resolution, inclusion of poetic elements) but they all guarantee the receivers' participation, thus stimulating their capacity to dismantle existing stereotypes and to resymbolize the real, which is a crucial act in that process of de-reconstruction of the cultural order that, according to Bourdieu, can destitute symbolic violence (2002:123). The literary origin of the aforementioned techniques, however, does not prevent authors from employing them in the context of journalistic narratives, as demonstrated by Iacona's and Maiorana's books, where the strategy of subjective narration is adopted despite the texts' general informative approach. Conversely, literary texts might not employ open narrative features, as in the case of *Fiore… come me*, where the dialog with journalistic practices results in a documental esthetics (Ricciardi 2011) that averts the writer from making the reader aware of her positioning and impedes any attempt at opening the text.

In light of this, hybridization between journalistic and literary practices is a desirable but not always beneficial tendency when it comes to the representation of femicide. On the one hand, hybridization allows journalism to abandon its long-standing pretentious objectivity and it permits literary portrayals to engage in a closer dialogue with the reality of the phenomenon. On the other hand, the uncontrolled osmosis of narrative practices and styles between the two spheres risks becoming detrimental to an ethical depiction of lethal gender violence. This is the case of fictionalization, which might contribute to the stereotyping of victims and perpetrators in texts on true events characterized by a prevalently informative approach, as we have seen in the analysis of Fiorucci's and Maiorana's works. In other words, fictionalization obstructs the possibility of assuring textual openness when not transparently applied or when employed in texts with a documentary ethics. On the contrary, texts, where fictional strategies are explicitly adopted, demonstrate a higher degree of openness and, consequently a better capacity of creatively overcoming the symbolic polarizations that authorize the social practice of sexist violence. This is because fair communication on the process of novelization of true events or on the inherently fictional character of the text guarantees more freedom to authors who want to experiment with the plot. As the analysis of works carried out in the second part of this study indicates, fiction and its implicit faculty to explore the dimension of the possible (Casadei 2007:119–120) are powerful tools against the naturalization of the female victim versus male perpetrator dichotomy proposed by patriarchal discourse and societal structures.

The volume includes texts written both by female and male authors. Following the analysis conducted in the previous pages, the gender identity of those who write affects the ethics of the narrative only in the case of autobiographical/autofictional works (Albinati's *La scuola cattolica*) or in the case of highly intersubjective narratives with a strong non-fictional component (Iacona's and Maiorana's books). In other cases, gender cannot prove to have a direct effect on the text, given the fact that fictional and non-intersubjective storytelling practices make the author transparent. Notwithstanding this, a general tendency of female authors to adopt a victim-centered approach and, conversely, a propensity of male authors to adopt a perpetrator-centered one was observed.

The range of books discussed consists of works with a limited or local circulation and reception (*Il sangue delle donne*, *Quello che resta*, *Fiore… come me*), texts published by national medium-size publishers and widely distributed or advertised (*Se questi sono gli uomini* and *Nessuna più*), and novels published by major Italian presses that received significant scholarly attention (*La scuola cattolica* and *Padreterno*). In light of this, the analysis considers a vast spectrum of publication typologies produced in Italy on the topic of femicide. However, the general impact that the studied narrative might have in a country like Italy, where only 40% of the population over six years of age read more than one book per year (ISTAT 2021:8), is necessarily not large. Not large but definitely not insignificant, if we consider that reading is a prevailing practice among school-age Italians (ISTAT 2021:8), the social group on which an action to contrast femicide culture is more needed and potentially more efficacious. That is why reading and knowing how to carefully select what we read or recommend to read can guide us toward the possibility of a future relieved from the imperative of sexist violence.

Works cited

Abis, S. and Orrù, P. (2016) "Il femminicidio nella stampa italiana: un'indagine linguistica," *Gender/sexuality/italy* 3: https://www.gendersexualityitaly.com/wp-content/uploads/2016/12/2.-Orru%CC%80-and-Abis.pdf. Accessed 2 January 2021.

Biaggioni, E. and Pirrone, M. (eds.) (2018) *L'attuazione della Convenzione di Istanbul in Italia. Rapporto delle associazioni di donne*: https://www.direcontrolaviolenza.it/wp-content/uploads/2018/10/GREVIO.Report.Ital_.finale-1.pdf. Accessed 22 January 2021.

Bourdieu, P. (2002) [1998] *Masculine Domination*. Trans. R. Nice. Bloomington: Stanford University Press.

Camilli, A. (2020) I fondi che mancano per combattere la violenza contro le donne. *Internazionale*. November 25: https://www.internazionale.it/reportage/annalisa-camilli/2020/11/25/centri-antiviolenza-fondi-femminicidi. Accessed 22 January 2021.

Casadei, A. (2007) *Stile e tradizione nel romanzo italiano contemporaneo*. Bologna: Il Mulino.

Cucklanz, L. (2000) *Rape on Prime Time: Television, Masculinity, and Sexual Violence*. Philadelphia: University of Pennsylvania Press.

D.i.Re. (2019) 4 milioni in più per I centri antiviolenza. 'Non bastano le risorse aggiuntive, vanno programmate e gestite,' *D.i.Re*. December 11: https://www.direcontrolaviolenza.it/4-milioni-in-piu-per-i-centri-antiviolenza-non-bastano-le-risorse-aggiuntive-vanno-programmate-e-gestite/. Accessed 22 January 2021.

Giomi, E. (2015) "Tag femminicidio. La violenza letale contro le donne nella stampa italiana," *Problemi dell'informazione* 50(3):549–574.

Giomi, E. (2019) "La rappresentazione della violenza di genere nei media. Frame, cause e soluzioni del problema nei programmi RAI," *Studi sulla questione criminale* 14(1-2):223–248.

Giomi, E. and Magaraggia, S. (2017) *Relazioni brutali. Genere e violenza nella cultura mediale*. Bologna: Il Mulino.

ISTAT (2021) *Produzione e lettura di libri in Italia. Anno 2019*: https://www.istat.it/it/files//2021/01/REPORT_LIBRI-REV_def.pdf. Accessed 25 January 2021.

Mandolini, N. (2020) "Femminicidio, prima e dopo. Un'analisi qualitativa della copertura giornalistica dei casi Stefania Noce (2011) e Sara Di Pietrantonio (2016)," *Problemi dell'informazione* 65(2):246–277.

Moorti, S. (2002) *Color of Rape: Gender and Race in Television's Public Spheres*. Albany: State University of New York Press.

Ricciardi, S. (2011) "'Gomorra' e l'estetica documentale nel nuovo millennio," *Interférences Littéraires* 7:167–186.

Rossitto, S. (2020) Eures: stabile il numero dei femminicidi nel 2020, effetto lockdown sulle vittime conviventi (+10,2%). *Il sole 24 ore*. November 25: https://www.ilsole24ore.com/art/eures-stabile-numero-femminicidi-2020-effetto-lockdown-vittime-conviventi-102percento-ADJAxL4. Accessed 22 January 2021.

Index

Note: Page numbers followed by n represent end notes.

For Product Safety Concerns and Information please contact our EU representative GPSR@taylorandfrancis.com
Taylor & Francis Verlag GmbH, Kaufingerstraße 24, 80331 München, Germany

www.ingramcontent.com/pod-product-compliance
Lightning Source LLC
LaVergne TN
LVHW020638100826
845148LV00012B/2227

* 9 7 8 0 3 6 7 6 3 6 9 9 9 *